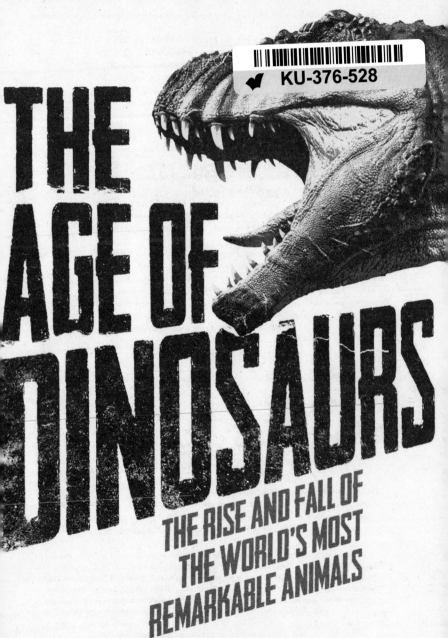

STEVE BRUSATTE

KU-376-528

THE AGE OF DINOSAURS

THE RISE AND FALL OF THE WORLD'S MOST REMARKABLE ANIMALS

MACMILLAN CHILDREN'S BOOKS

First published in the US 2021 by Quill Tree Books, an imprint of HarperCollins Publishers

First published 2021 by Macmillan Children's Books
an imprint of Macmillan Publishers Limited
The Smithson, 6 Briset Street, London EC1M 5NR
EU representative: Macmillan Publishers Ireland Limited,
Mallard Lodge, Lansdowne Village, Dublin 4
Associated companies throughout the world
www.panmacmillan.com

ISBN 978-1-5290-1741-0

Text copyright © Steve Brusatte 2021
Interior art copyright © Todd Marshall

The right of Steve Brusatte and Todd Marshall to be
identified as the author and illustrator of this work has been asserted by them
in accordance with the Copyright, Designs and Patents Act 1988.

1 3 5 7 9 8 6 4 2

A CIP catalogue record for this book is available from the British Library.

Printed and bound by CPI Group (UK) Ltd, Croydon CR0 4YY

Grateful acknowledgment is given to the following sources for the images in this book:
Page 22: Photographer: Sharat Ganapati (Creative Commons); page 25: Cecilia Apaldetti; page 29:
Cecilia Apaldetti; page 51–52: US Geological Survey; page 71: AMNH Research Library, photographer
Kay C. Lenskjold; page 71: John Ostrom/Peabody Museum (public domain); page 74: PLoS ONE
(Creative Commons); page 93: Photographer: Tim Evanson (Creative Commons); page 127: Sara Burch;
page 139: Scott Williams; page 145: Ali Nabavizadeh; page 152: Adrienne Mayor; page 153: Across
Mongolian Plains: A Naturalist's Account of China's "Great Northwest" (public domain); page 178:
Eigen archief (public domain); page 185: Mick Ellison; page 214: NASA.
All other photos are courtesy of the author.

To Ms Schultz, Mrs Roberts, Mrs Boam,
and all of my science teachers –
and all of my teachers –
at Wallace Grade School in Ottawa, Illinois.
Thanks for teaching me about the world
beyond the cornfields, and for reading all of
those stories and 'books' I wrote . . .

Contents

TIME

Era	Paleozoic		Mesozoic	
Period	Permian	Triassic	Jurassic	
Epoch		Early	Middle	Late	Early	Middle
Age (millions of years ago)		252 – 247	247 – 237	237 – 201	201 – 174	174 – 164

Cenozoic

Cretaceous

Paleogene

Late

Early

Late

Late

ix

~ 145

145 – 100

100 – 66

Permian Period

299–252 million years ago: Before the dinosaurs, when mammal ancestors and other reptiles and amphibians ruled the world

Triassic Period

252 million years ago: End-Permian mass extinction

250 million years ago: First fossils of the dinosaur lineage: *Prorotodactylus* tracks from Poland

230 million years ago: Oldest true dinosaurs: *Herrerasaurus, Eoraptor, Eodromaeus,* and other species from Ischigualasto, Argentina

215 million years ago: The first giant dinosaur: *Ingentia* from Argentina

212 million years ago: Dinosaurs remain rare and less successful than the pseudosuchians and giant salamanders, as shown by the Hayden Quarry fossils

201 million years ago: Pangea begins to split and the end-Triassic mass extinction occurs

Jurassic Period

200–170 million years ago: Dinosaurs become larger, spread around the world, and become dominant

170 million years ago: Giant long-necked sauropods roam the lagoons of Skye, Scotland

170 million years ago: Tyrannosaurs originate as small, second-tier predators

DIN

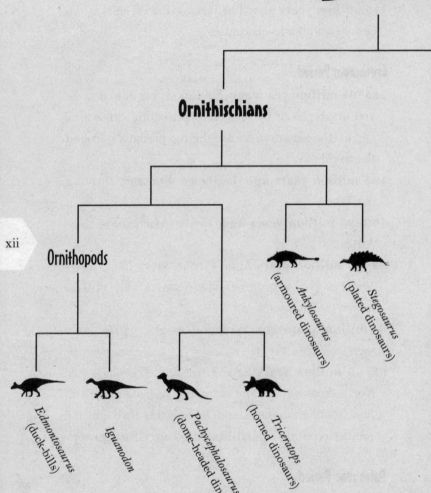

Ornithischians

Ornithopods

Ankylosaurus
(armoured dinosaurs)

Stegosaurus
(plated dinosaurs)

Edmontosaurus
(duck-bills)

Iguanodon

Pachycephalosaurus
(dome-headed dinos)

Triceratops
(horned dinosaurs)

SAURS

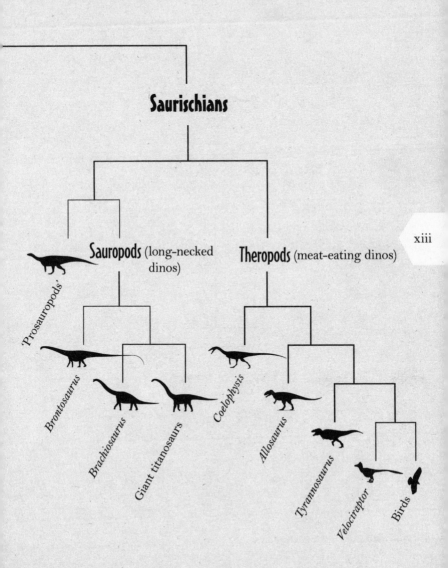

Saurischians

Sauropods (long-necked dinos)

Theropods (meat-eating dinos)

'Prosauropods'

Brontosaurus

Brachiosaurus

Giant titanosaurs

Coelophysis

Allosaurus

Tyrannosaurus

Velociraptor

Birds

Introduction

A few years ago, on a cold November morning, I got out of a taxi and entered the railway station in Beijing, the capital city of China. The station was packed with people on their way to work. I was there for work too. I am a paleontologist, a scientist who studies fossils – the remains of ancient plants and animals – so I can understand what Earth was like millions of years ago, long before humans were alive. I had travelled to China from my home in Scotland to see a secret new fossil – the skeleton of a dinosaur! – that had just been discovered by a farmer.

I met my friend Junchang Lü, who had invited me to come to China and help him study this new mystery dinosaur. I was still a young scientist. Only a couple of years earlier, I had finished my PhD degree. Junchang, however, was a famous professor. He had discovered and named dozens of new dinosaur species, and he was often on television. Junchang and I had worked together many times, studying many dinosaurs.

'We need to go now!' Junchang yelled to me as he pointed to a train behind him, which was starting up its engines.

We both ran on to the train, and for the next four hours, we crawled past concrete factories and hazy cornfields in the countryside of China. Occasionally I nodded off, but I couldn't sleep much. I was far too excited! I had seen a few photos of the mystery dinosaur, and I knew it would be special.

Finally, the train stopped at our destination: the city of Jinzhou, in the Liaoning province at the far northeastern corner of China.

Junchang and I were met by a group of local citizens, who immediately took us to the city's museum, a plain building on the edge of town. It all felt very thrilling, like we were part of a secret undercover mission. And in a sense, we were: nobody except for us, and the farmer, knew about this dinosaur skeleton. Inside the museum, there was a 125-million-year-old fossil, and we would be the first people to ever study it.

Once through the museum doors, we were led down a long hallway with flickering neon lights, and then into a side room with a couple of desks and chairs. A slab of rock was balanced on a small table, so heavy that it looked like the table might collapse. One of the locals spoke in Chinese to Junchang, who then turned to me and gave a quick nod.

'Let's go,' he said.

The two of us stepped towards the table and approached the treasure.

I was astonished. In front of me was one of the most beautiful fossils I had ever seen. The skeleton was about the size of a mule, with chocolate-brown bones standing out from the dull grey rock surrounding it. It was a dinosaur for sure. Its steak-knife-sharp teeth, pointy claws, and long tail immediately showed that it was a close

Junchang Lü and Steve Brusatte studying the fossil of Zhenyuanlong.

cousin of *Velociraptor*, the villain from *Jurassic Park*.

But this was no ordinary dinosaur. Its bones were light and hollow, and its legs long and skinny. Its slender skeleton clearly belonged to an active, fast-moving animal. And not only were there bones, but there were feathers covering the entire body. Bushy feathers that looked like hair on the head and neck, long branching feathers on the tail, and big quills on the arms, lined together and layered over each other to form wings.

This dinosaur looked just like a bird!

About a year later, Junchang and I described this skeleton as a new species, which we called *Zhenyuanlong*.

It is one of about fifteen new dinosaurs that I've identified over the past decade, as I've enjoyed a career that has taken me from my roots in the American Midwest to my job teaching at the University of Edinburgh in Scotland, with many stops all over the world to find and study dinosaurs.

Zhenyuanlong is unlike the dinosaurs I learned about in primary school. I was taught that dinosaurs were big, scale-covered, stupid animals that lived in an ancient world that was totally different from today's Earth. The books I read when I was young often called dinosaurs 'failures', because they died out or went extinct. Many people told me that dinosaurs were not important to learn about, and that studying them was a waste of time.

But all these ideas are wrong!

We now know that dinosaurs were remarkably successful, thriving for more than 150 million years. They were some of the most amazing animals that ever lived: some species became larger than jet airplanes, and others developed into today's birds (meaning that dinosaurs are not actually extinct!). The dinosaurs lived on the same Earth that we now live on, and they had to deal with many things: volcanic eruptions, asteroid impacts, the land moving around, sea levels rising and falling, temperatures getting hotter and colder. The dinosaurs were always changing and adapting.

How do we know this? Because paleontologists are

discovering so many new dinosaur fossils, and are using new technologies to study them.

Somewhere around the world – from the deserts of Argentina to the icelands of Alaska – a new species of dinosaur is currently being found, on average, once a week. Let that sink in: a new dinosaur every ... single ... week. That's about fifty new species each year – *Zhenyuanlong* among them.

Why are there so many new dinosaur discoveries? The answer is simple. There are more people looking for dinosaurs than ever before, all over the world. It used to be that paleontology was a strange career, and was mostly limited to a few people who worked at big universities or museums in the United States, Canada, and western Europe. But now there are large communities of young scientists in China, Argentina, Brazil, and so many other countries. People also used to think that dinosaurs were a 'boy thing'. Little boys would be encouraged to learn about dinosaurs, but girls often were not. Thankfully, that has changed too.

Paleontologists like me also have many high-tech ways of studying dinosaurs in our laboratories. We use CAT scanners, just like medical doctors do, to X-ray the inside of dinosaur skulls to study the brain and ears. We use computer animation software, just like movie-makers and video-game designers do, to study how dinosaurs moved. We even use high-powered microscopes to examine the skin and feathers of dinosaurs, which can tell us what color these dinosaurs were when they were alive. All these technologies help us understand dinosaurs as real living, breathing, moving, growing animals.

I love my job. Being a paleontologist is like being a detective. With each new discovery, each new study, we learn a little more about dinosaurs and their incredible story.

That is the story I am going to tell in this book. It is the story of dinosaur evolution: how dinosaurs changed over time as their world changed around them. It is an epic tale of where dinosaurs came from, how they spread around the world and became dominant, how some of them became huge and others developed feathers and wings and turned into birds, and then how the rest of them disappeared when the environment suddenly changed. In doing so, I want to explain how we've pieced together this story using the fossil clues that we have, and show what it's like to be a paleontologist whose job it is to hunt for dinosaurs.

The rise and fall of the dinosaurs is an incredible story, and I think there is a lot that we can learn from the dinosaurs.

Steve Brusatte
Edinburgh, Scotland

1

The Ancestors of the Dinosaurs

Prorotodactylus

'Bingo,' my friend paleontologist Grzegorz Niedźwiedzki shouted, pointing at a cliff. His fingers traced the line where a strip of shale (rock hardened from ancient mud) connected with a much thicker layer of conglomerate (rock made up of pebbles and boulders glued together).

Grzegorz and I were exploring an abandoned limestone quarry in the tiny village of Zachełmie, Poland. The sky was grey, the mosquitoes were biting, and the wind made a strange, lonely noise.

'This is the extinction line,' Grzegorz said with a big smile. 'There are many footprints of big reptiles and mammal cousins below, in the shale rock, but then they disappear. And above, we see no fossils in the conglomerate rock, but then afterwards come the dinosaurs.'

Grzegorz determined this by carefully studying the rocks, because rocks record history. Different rocks form in different types of climates and environments, and a skilled geologist – a scientist who studies rocks – can look at them and envision what the world was like when they formed. Sandstone, for instance, might have formed on a sandy beach. Mudstone could have been made from the mud by the side of a lake. A conglomerate might come from the layer of pebbles on the bottom of a fast-moving river.

Rocks are also important to paleontologists because fossils, like dinosaur bones, are found inside rocks.

Follow the fossils, find the clues

Fossils are a sign of ancient life, and they come in many forms. The most familiar are bones, teeth, and shells – the hard parts that form the skeleton of an animal. After being buried in sand or mud, these hard bits are gradually replaced by minerals and turned into rock, leaving a fossil. Sometimes soft things, like leaves, can fossilize as well, often by making impressions in the rock. The same is sometimes true of the soft parts of animals, like skin, feathers, or even muscles. But to capture these as fossils, we need to be very lucky: the animal needs to be buried so quickly that these fragile tissues don't have time to break down or decay or get eaten by predators.

Everything described above is what we call a *body fossil*, an actual part of a plant or an animal that turns into stone. But there is another type of fossil, a *trace fossil*, which records the behavior of an animal, or is something that an animal produced. The best example of a trace fossil is a footprint, but others are burrows, bite marks, coprolites (fossilized poo!), and eggs and nests. These can be very valuable because they can tell us how prehistoric animals interacted with each other and their environment – how they moved, what they ate, where they lived, and how they reproduced.

You can think of fossils as clues, and you can think of paleontologists as detectives. A police detective might go to a crime scene and collect fingerprints, hairs, and other evidence to help understand how a crime was committed. Similarly, a paleontologist collects fossils to identify plants and animals that used to be alive, and use them to study and understand their world.

Paleontologists Steve Brusatte and Richard Butler search for fossils at a site in Poland.

The fossils that I'm most interested in belong to dinosaurs and the animals that came immediately before and after them. Dinosaurs lived during three periods of ancient history – the Triassic, Jurassic, and Creta-ceous periods. Together, these three periods form the

Mesozoic Era – the so-called Age of Dinosaurs. The Triassic Period began about 252 million years ago, and the Cretaceous Period ended about 66 million years ago. Everything in between was the Age of Dinosaurs.

In the beginning . . .

We often think of the dinosaurs as being very, very old. And they are. But there were many things that lived long before the dinosaurs.

The Earth is incredibly ancient. Our planet formed 4.6 billion years ago out of a ball of dust and gas. The first tiny bacteria evolved a few hundred million years later. Then, for about two billion years, bacteria ruled the world. They were the only living species; there were no plants and animals. These came much later, about 600 million years ago. At first, animals were simple – just soft sacs of goo, like sponges and jellyfish. But then they evolved shells and skeletons, which allowed them to better protect themselves. Some animals developed an internal skeleton of bone. These animals, called vertebrates, kept evolving, first swimming in the water as fish, and then some developing arms and legs and moving on to the land, about 390 million years ago. The descendants of these land-colonizing fish include all vertebrates that live on land today: frogs and salamanders, crocodiles and snakes, and then later dinosaurs, and even us.

Rocks tell the story

We know this story because of fossils, and the rocks that contain the fossils. Paleontologists like me are obsessed with finding fossils, and we often go to great lengths to discover new ones. We might head into the desert or up a steep mountain to find fossils, but other times we can find them alongside streams or where construction workers cut into the ground to build roads. Sometimes we just have to go into a rock quarry, which is exactly what Grzegorz and I were doing in Poland.

Why did we choose this particular quarry? If we want to find fossils, we need to look in rocks of the right age and the right type. The rocks there were formed about 252 million years ago, right as the Triassic Period – and the Age of Dinosaurs – was beginning. These rocks tell the story of a terrible environmental crisis that ultimately led to a worldwide mass extinction, which is a short period of time when a huge number of plants and animals die out all at once. And most important, the rocks in this Polish quarry contain lots and lots of fossils.

We can't just go digging in our backyards and expect to find dinosaurs. Instead, we look at maps produced by geologists, which show the types of rocks that are exposed on the surface of the Earth. We locate places with rocks that formed during the Mesozoic Era, in environments that dinosaurs lived in. So, for example, we might target a Jurassic-aged mudstone that formed on the edge of a lake. But we would never look in a two-billion-year-old basalt rock formed by a volcano – these rocks are far too old to contain dinosaur bones, and they formed in a fiery environment that dinosaurs would never live in.

And then, when we find suitable rocks on the geology maps, we simply go to those places, walk around, and look for fossils sticking out of the ground! There is no fancy equipment, no radar or sonar that helps us see inside the rocks. We just use our eyes. This means that we always need good luck, as well as patience.

Grzegorz knew that the rocks in this quarry were perfect for finding fossils. He grew up in this part of central Poland, the Holy Cross Mountains, and started collecting fossils as a child. He developed a talent for finding trace fossils like footprints and handprints.

An animal has only one skeleton, but can leave millions of footprints

The footprints in the quarry tell an amazing story of change over time. The first footprints, found in the mudstone rocks near the floor of the quarry, were made by animals living in the Permian Period, the time right before the Mesozoic Era, before dinosaurs existed. It was a time even before there were separate continents like today. There was no North America or Africa.

Instead, all the land was joined together into one giant 'supercontinent' called Pangea, which was surrounded by a single ocean called Panthalassa.

Imagine if we were standing where the quarry is now, but 252 million years ago, during the very end of the Permian Period. There would have been no birds in the sky, no squirrels in the trees, and no flowers or grass. We would have been sweating because it was hot and very humid, probably similar to the climate in Florida or Spain today. Raging rivers drained the Holy Cross Mountains, which jutted high into the clouds. The rivers wound their way through thick forests of conifer trees – early relatives of today's pine trees – before emptying into a giant lake.

And this lake was the centre of life. Many fish swam in its crystal-blue waters, and many other animals flocked to its edge. We would not recognize these animals, though. There were slimy salamanders bigger than dogs, stocky reptiles called pareiasaurs that waddled on all four legs, and plump reptiles called dicynodonts that used their sharp tusks to dig up roots to eat. All these animals lived in fear of the gorgonopsians, bear-sized hunters that used their long, sharp canine teeth to kill their prey. These were the animals that ruled the Polish lake, and the entire world of Pangea, right before the dinosaurs. We know that because we find so many of their footprints in Poland and all over the world.

Then something changed

The Earth began to rumble deep inside. Currents of magma – hot liquid rock – started to flow upward and burst out of volcanoes in what is now Russia. These were not ordinary volcanoes, like the cone-shaped hills that sometimes erupt today. Instead, these were *megavolcanoes*: big cracks in the Earth, often miles long, which continuously released lava (what magma is called when it reaches the Earth's surface) for hundreds of thousands of years. The lava covered several million square miles of northern and central Asia, which is about the same as the area of modern-day Europe.

But the lava wasn't the biggest problem. When volcanoes erupt, they also release poisonous gases like carbon dioxide and methane. These are greenhouse gases: they help the atmosphere keep in heat, which in turn makes the Earth warmer. At the end of the Permian Period, these gases caused the Earth to get warmer by about 10 degrees Celsius (50 degrees Fahrenheit), which was a *huge* temperature increase in such a short amount of time. Plants and animals could not cope with such rapid change. Therefore, a mass extinction occurred. Around 95 per cent of all species died out! This was the largest single period of dying in Earth's history. It was the closest life has ever come to completely dying out.

A new beginning

Most of those animals that lived in that Polish lake died. But over time, the volcanoes stopped erupting. The temperature returned to normal. Plants started to grow again. The surviving animals came out of their burrows and found themselves with a nearly empty world to explore.

The mass extinction marks the end of the Permian Period and the beginning of the Triassic Period – and thus the Mesozoic Era. The Age of Dinosaurs was just beginning.

Among the few survivors of the extinction was a small type of reptile. We don't know much about it because we haven't found its fossils yet. But we have found handprints and footprints of one of its descendants, an animal that was living near the Polish lakes just one or two million years after the volcanoes erupted. These tracks go by the name of *Prorotodactylus.*

The *Prorotodactylus* tracks are small – just about an inch (2–3 centimeters) long – about the size of a cat's paw. They are arranged in trackways (the sequence of handprints

A handprint overlapping a footprint of Prorotodactylus.

and footprints), with the handprints positioned in front of the slightly larger footprints. The handprints have five fingers, while the footprints have three long toes in the middle, with a tiny toe on each side.

The best place to find these tracks is near a tiny Polish village called Stryczowice, which is not too far from the quarry in Zachełmie. Grzegorz discovered the site when he was a teenager, and he took me there during one of my trips to Poland. It was a hot July day, full of rain and thunder. We parked our car at a bridge, scrambled through thornbushes, and finally came to a narrow stream. Layers of mudstone rock poked out of the stream, surrounded by swarms of mosquitoes. By this point we were very wet, but we went up to the rocks. I became very excited when we found new *Prorotodactylus* tracks!

Whose tracks are they?

But what type of animal made the *Prorotodactylus* tracks? To answer this question, we needed to compare the handprints and footprints to the hands and feet of fossil skeletons to see what animal has the closest match to the footprints.

When I looked at the tracks, I noticed that the trackways are very narrow; there is very little space between the left and right hands, and the left and right feet. There is only one way for an animal to make tracks like this: it has to be walking upright, with the arms and legs underneath its body. Humans walk upright, so when we leave footprints on the beach, the left and right ones are very close together. Other mammals like horses and cows walk upright too. But this style of walking is actually very rare in the animal kingdom. Salamanders, frogs, and lizards move in a different way. Their arms and legs stick out sideways from the body. This is called *sprawling*, meaning their trackways are much wider, with big separation between the left and right hands and the left and right feet.

Does this mean that *Prorotodactylus* was a mammal, perhaps a close relative of humans? No, because there were other animals that evolved an upright way of walking during the Triassic Period, long before humans. They are a type of reptile called archosaurs. By tucking their limbs under their bodies, these archosaurs were able to run faster, cover greater distances, and track down prey more easily. Their limbs wasted less energy by moving back and forth in a simple manner, rather than the twisting way that a sprawler has to walk.

In the earliest part of the Triassic Period, after the volcanoes stopped erupting, the archosaurs began to thrive. They split into two major groups, which both survive today. The first group includes crocodiles and their extinct relatives. The second includes pterosaurs (the flying reptiles also known as pterodactyls), dinosaurs, and today's birds (which descended from the dinosaurs).

Prorotodactylus was an archosaur, but what type of archosaur was it?

14

Two Prorotodactylus *dinosaurs – close dinosaur cousins*

Some strange features in the footprints provide the answer. Only the toes make an impression in the rock, not the metatarsal bones that form the arch of the foot. The three central toes are bunched very close together, and the two other toes are so small that they are almost absent. The back end of the footprint is straight and razor sharp. These are all features of dinosaurs and their very closest relatives!

We see the same things in the foot skeletons of dinosaurs and their closest cousins. These animals have a digitigrade foot – that means that they walk on their toes, like ballerinas. They have a very narrow foot in which the central toes are bunched together. They have a foot with three main toes in the middle, and reduced or absent outer toes. And they have a simple hinge-like ankle joint, which can only move back and forth like a flap. This is why the back end of the *Prorotodactylus* tracks is so straight.

So what does it all mean?

This means that *Prorotodactylus* is in the dinosaur group! In strict scientific terms, it is a *dinosauromorph*, meaning it is a member of the group that includes true dinosaurs and their very closest cousins. In the next chapter, I will explain in more detail how a true dinosaur differs from a dinosauromorph. But for now, this is what you need to know: *Prorotodactylus* is basically an ancestor of the dinosaurs. And by studying *Prorotodactylus*, we can understand what types of animals dinosaurs evolved from.

If we could see *Prorotodactylus* alive, we probably wouldn't be very impressed. It wasn't nearly as big as a *Brontosaurus* or as scary as a *T. rex*. It would have been a very simple and humble animal, about the size of a house cat and probably weighing around 10 pounds (4.5 kilograms). It walked on all four legs, and both its arms and legs were very long. Its small hands were good at grabbing things, and its long feet were perfect for running. It was also a very rare animal. Less than 5 per cent of the total tracks found at Stryczowice belong to *Prorotodactylus*. It is found alongside many more tracks of small reptiles, amphibians, and crocodile relatives.

But *Prorotodactylus* was only the beginning. As the Triassic Period continued to unfold and the world continued to heal from the end-Permian megavolcanoes, the dinosauromorphs continued to evolve. They got bigger, they spread around most of the world, and some started to walk on only their hind legs. Most of them ate meat, but some of them turned vegetarian. They moved quickly, grew fast, ate a lot of food, and were much more active and dynamic than the sprawling reptiles they lived alongside.

And then, at some point in the middle part of the Triassic Period, these dinosauromorphs gave rise to the dinosaurs.

16

2

Dinosaurs Appear

Herrerasaurus

TIMELINE: Middle-Late Triassic

ca. 230 million years ago

Paleontologists find fossils all over the world. While the *Prorotodactylus* footprints were discovered in Poland, the oldest dinosaurs are found in Argentina, South America. These dinosaurs lived about 230 million years ago and there were many different species, including *Herrerasaurus, Eoraptor, Eocursor,* and *Panphagia*. And while there are similarities among them, there are also distinct differences.

What makes a dinosaur a dinosaur?

Scientists classify animals based on the features they have. For example, mice, tigers, monkeys, and humans are all classified as mammals because we share the same characteristics. All mammals have hair, produce milk to feed their young, and have two sets of teeth in their lifetime (baby teeth while young and permanent teeth as an adult).

Dinosaurs do not have any of these things, but they share their own set of unique features. They all have a pelvis with a large open hole where the thighbone attaches, which helps them stand up straighter and taller. They all have extra backbones (vertebrae) in their hips, to attach their pelvis bones more securely to their back. And they all have a long ridge of bone on their upper arm that anchors powerful muscles, which four-legged species used to run and two-legged species used to grab prey.

The animal that made the *Prorotodactylus* tracks in Poland did not have these features, so it is not a dinosaur. But the species from Argentina did, so they are considered to be dinosaurs. *T. rex*, *Brontosaurus*, *Triceratops*, and *Stegosaurus* also have these traits, so they are dinosaurs too.

You can think of it this way: *T. rex*, *Brontosaurus*, *Triceratops*, *Stegosaurus*, and the many thousands of other dinosaur species are like sisters and brothers in one big dinosaur family. *Prorotodactylus* is their cousin.

How do we know how old these dinosaurs are?

Throughout this book, I will talk a lot about time. I will tell you, for example, that a particular dinosaur lived 230 million years ago, or that a certain mass extinction happened 66 million years ago. But how do I know these dates?

Again, the rocks tell the story! Not only do rocks contain fossils, so we can see these dinosaur families, but we also can determine how old each fossil is. Geologists can figure out the age of some rocks by measuring the types of chemicals the rocks are made of. This is called *radioisotopic dating*.

WHAT IS RADIOISOTOPIC DATING?

When a rock cools from a liquid into a solid – like when hot lava cools into basalt rock – mineral crystals form. Some crystals are made of special elements, which over time change into other elements. One example is potassium, which changes into argon. As time passes, the crystals lose more and more of their potassium and become more full of argon. We know the speed at which potassium changes into argon because we can measure it in the lab today. Therefore, if we take a rock, we can measure the percentage of potassium and the percentage of argon, and then use a math equation to calculate how long ago the rock formed.

But there is one problem when it comes to dinosaurs. Radioisotopic dating works only on rocks that cool from lava. However, dinosaur fossils are usually found in rocks like mudstone and sandstone, which formed from water currents in lakes and rivers. Dating these rocks is much more difficult, so paleontologists have to be creative. Sometimes, we find small crystals alongside dinosaur bones. These crystals formed in volcanoes and were buried with the dinosaur. We can date the crystal and get the age of the dinosaur. Other times, we find dinosaur bones in a layer of mudstone sandwiched between two layers of lava rock. In this case, we can date the lava rocks above and below the dinosaur bones, and we will know the dinosaur must have lived during this span of time.

The oldest dinosaurs of Argentina

Herrerasaurus – *one of the oldest dinosaurs in Argentina*

There is a beautiful place in Argentina called Ischigualasto Provincial Park, also known as Valle de la Luna, which means the Valley of the Moon. It is a perfect name for this strange, almost spooky land of colourful rock layers that are sculpted into cliffs, canyons, and hills. Not many people live in this harsh desert, but for centuries, Ischigualasto has been an important crossing point for farmers, who bring herds of cattle from the mountains of Chile across to the grassy plains of central and southern Argentina.

Some of these same farmers discovered the first dinosaur fossils inside the red, brown, and green rocks that were formed during the middle part of the Triassic Period. These rocks were made in an environment similar to the one *Prorotodactylus* lived in. This may seem strange, because Argentina is very far from Poland today. But remember, during the Triassic Period, all the land was connected into the supercontinent of Pangea.

If you could imagine yourself in Argentina 230 million years ago, the climate would have been hot and humid. Rivers flowed across the land, emptying into a deep lake. Over millions of years, the rivers built up layers of sandstone and mudstone on the surrounding plains during floods. Many dinosaurs frolicked on these plains, along with many other animals – big amphibians, piglike dicynodonts whose ancestors made it through the end-Permian extinction, plant-eating reptiles with beaks called rhynchosaurs, and furry little cynodonts (primitive mammal ancestors) that looked like a cross between a rat and an iguana. Floods would occasionally interrupt this paradise, killing the dinosaurs and their friends and burying their bones.

Discoveries

Once farmers began finding bones in Ischigualasto,

scientists started to visit. The first major fieldwork happened in the 1940s and 1950s. As was often the case at the time, it was not local scientists who did most of the work. Rather, Alfred Romer, a prominent American paleontologist, was in charge. During a visit in 1958, Romer found part of a skull and a skeleton of a dinosaur. This discovery motivated two young Argentine paleontologists, Osvaldo Reig and José Bonaparte, to organize their own expeditions. By working with locals who knew the area well, they found many more dinosaurs.

Their most important discovery was a skeleton found by the farmer Victorino Herrera. It was a horse-sized animal with sharp teeth and claws. Reig studied the skeleton and named it *Herrerasaurus* in the farmer's honor.

24

The hand of a Herrerasaurus *dinosaur, one of the oldest dinosaurs*

You can think of *Herrerasaurus* as a smaller version of *T. rex*. It was fast, fierce, and agile. It ran around only on its hind legs, and used its arms to grab prey. It has all the trademark features of dinosaurs – the open pelvis, the extra backbones, the large muscles on the arms – which means it is a true dinosaur! Today, we recognize *Herrerasaurus* as one of the very first dinosaurs. Not only that, but it is a theropod dinosaur: a member of the group of meat-eaters that includes *T. rex*, *Velociraptor*, *Allosaurus*, and many other famous hunters. Basically, *Herrerasaurus* is the great-great-great-great-grandparent of *T. rex*!

IT TAKES A TEAM

Ricardo Martinez and Cecilia Apaldetti's team working in an Ischigualasto bone bed.

Today, a large team of Argentine scientists, including Ricardo Martínez and Cecilia Apaldetti, continues the work of Reig and Bonaparte. Ricardo began collecting fossils in Ischigualasto in the 1980s. Then later, in the 2000s, Cecilia became his student. Today, she is one of the leading dinosaur hunters in the world. They have found and studied many of the most important dinosaur skeletons from Ischigualasto, and are finding new fossils in other parts of Argentina.

When Ricardo was a student, he discovered something amazing. While walking in Ischigualasto one day, he picked up a fist-sized chunk of rock, which was covered with strange mineral crystals. He was just about to throw the rock aside when he noticed something pointy and shiny sticking out of one side.

It was teeth!

He realized that he had plucked the head off a dinosaur skeleton. But this was a different dinosaur than *Herrerasaurus*. It was much smaller, only the size of a large dog. It had a skinny body, long legs, and arms capped with sharp claws. Its teeth were very strange: the ones in the back of the jaw were sharp and had serrations for cutting, like a steak knife. They must have been used to slice through meat. But the ones at the tip of the snout were leaf-shaped, with big bumps called denticles. We know from modern animals that these teeth are perfect for grinding leaves and stems and are used for eating plants, not meat.

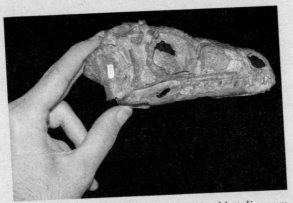

The skull of Eoraptor, *one of the oldest dinosaurs in the world*

Ricardo and his colleagues named their new dinosaur *Eoraptor*. It was an omnivore, meaning that it ate many different types of food. *Eoraptor* is not a theropod dinosaur like *Herrerasaurus*. Instead, it is one of the oldest members of another major group of dinosaurs, the sauropodomorphs. This is the group of omnivores and plant-eaters that also includes the largest dinosaurs that ever lived: the long-necked giants like *Brontosaurus*.

New species

There are also many other dinosaur species that have been discovered in Ischigualasto, including two other theropods: *Eodromaeus*, which is about the size of a cat, and *Sanjuansaurus*, which is very similar to *Herrerasaurus*. There are also several sauropodomorphs, like *Eoraptor* (see p.27), the wolf-sized *Panphagia*, and six-foot-long *Chromogisaurus*. Sauropodomorphs are a major group that also include the largest dinosaurs like *Brontosaurus*, *Brachiosaurus*, and *Diplodocus*.

As you can see, Ischigualasto was very diverse! Some dinosaurs here ate meat, some ate plants, some ate a variety of foods. Some were theropods, others were sauropodomorphs. By dating the rocks these dinosaurs are found in, Ricardo and his team can tell that they all lived together at the same time, about 230 million years ago.

This means that by the middle part of the Triassic Period, there were many different dinosaurs. These dinosaurs were mostly small and simple; they were not yet at the top of the food chain. But their evolutionary story was just beginning!

If you compare the dinosaurs of Ischigualasto to dinosaurs that came later, during the Jurassic and Cretaceous periods, something weird stands out. None of the Ischigualasto dinosaurs were very big. Dinosaurs like *T. rex* and *Brontosaurus* are famous because of their huge sizes, but the largest Ischigualasto dinosaur was only about the size of a horse.

So, when did dinosaurs start to become big? Cecilia Apaldetti (see p.26-27) figured it out. In 2018 she announced a remarkable discovery – a new Triassic dinosaur from Argentina. But this dinosaur comes from a different part of Argentina, south of Ischigualasto.

And it was found in rocks that formed about 215 million years ago, around 15 million years *after* the Ischigualasto dinosaurs lived.

Ingentia

Cecilia called this new dinosaur *Ingentia*, and it was a sauropodomorph, like *Eoraptor*, *Panphagia*, and *Chromogisaurus* from Ischigualasto. But it was so much larger! *Ingentia* was around 30 feet (9 metres) long and weighed about 10 tons. That's the same size as two Asian elephants put together! *Ingentia* grew fast and had enormous muscles along its backbone to help support its bulky size.

While *Ingentia* was nowhere near the size of the largest sauropodomorphs like *Brontosaurus*, which many millions of years later would grow even bigger than jet airplanes, this dinosaur was the starting point.

Dinosaurs were diversifying in the Triassic Period. They were changing, adapting, and starting to become giants.

And the dinosaurs were on the march!

3

Dinosaurs Rise Up

Coelophysis

TIMELINE: Late Triassic

ca. 230–200 million years ago

Paleontologists used to think that the dinosaurs were superior to other species living at the same time, that they quickly took over the world because they were bigger, stronger, and more successful than the other Triassic animals. But now we know this is not true.

If you were alive back in the Triassic Period and lived on the supercontinent of Pangea, you would have seen dinosaurs. Because of the fossils from Argentina, we know that dinosaurs lived during the Triassic. We know that there were meat-eaters and plant-eaters, and that some were starting to become big.

But if you were a Triassic time traveller, you probably would not be very impressed by the dinosaurs. Most of them wouldn't look very special. They were not yet dominant, not yet at the top of the food chain. Nothing as scary as *T. rex* or as large as *Brontosaurus* or as extraordinary as a three-horned *Triceratops* existed yet. Dinosaurs were there, but they were not the largest animals, or the most common animals, or the most successful animals. They did not yet rule the world.

What animals dominated the water?

Instead, there were other animals more powerful than

dinosaurs that reigned during the Triassic Period. And over many tens of millions of years, the dinosaurs would compete with these animals, and eventually defeat them. This battle lasted for the entire Triassic Period, from the time of the first dinosaurs in Argentina 230 million years ago until the end of the Triassic, 200 million years ago.

So what were these other animals? My colleagues Octávio Mateus and Richard Butler and I discovered a graveyard of their skeletons in Portugal.

Supersalamander site in Portugal

These creatures were amphibians – ancient cousins of today's salamanders: slimy creatures that lay eggs, grow up as tadpoles, and then live in wet environments, often at the boundary between water and land.

The fossils looked very similar to many salamanders that live today, but with one difference: they were much bigger. Each Portuguese amphibian was the size of a small car! Each one had a head with hundreds of sharp teeth that it would use to eat fish, other amphibians, or even dinosaurs. If that is not terrifying enough, these 'supersalamanders' lived in flocks of hundreds or thousands of individuals. They would have dominated the rivers and the lakes during much of the Triassic Period.

THE SUPERSALAMANDERS

When I was finishing my master's degree and about to start studying for my PhD, my friend Richard Butler sent me an email. Richard is a British paleontologist, and the two of us were looking for new places in Europe where we could search for fossils. He found a short report written by German paleontologists, describing a few pieces of bone from Triassic-aged rocks in the southern part of Portugal. These bones were picked up by a college geology student in the 1970s, when he was in Portugal doing a student project. He brought the bones back to a museum in Berlin, where they sat in a drawer for several decades. The reason nobody paid much attention to them was simple: they were just a few badly preserved, broken, puzzling pieces of bone. They were scrap.

But even the smallest clues can eventually reveal an amazing story. Richard and I felt that there were probably more bones – maybe even skeletons – hidden inside the rocks of Portugal, waiting to be found. So we contacted another friend of ours, Octávio Mateus, who ran a museum in Lourinhã, a town on the windy Atlantic coast of Portugal. His parents were amateur archaeologists and historians who'd started the museum many decades before. They trained Octávio to find fossils, and quickly he became the best dinosaur collector in all of Portugal.

Octávio, Richard, and I met in the hot August sun.

Octávio Mateus, Richard Butler, and Steve Brusatte at the supersalamander site in Portugal

Before we met up, we all did our homework. We went to the library and looked online for any information we could find: maps of the local geology, reports written by Portuguese geologists, descriptions of the local rocks. We found the place on the map where the German student found the bone scraps: it was called Penina, and located in the middle of a hilly, dry region about 20 miles from the ocean. The hills were carved out of Triassic-aged rocks that formed around the same time as the rocks in Ischigualasto, in which the oldest dinosaurs were found. We were very excited: maybe we would find Triassic-aged dinosaurs in Portugal too!

For several days we hiked through the sun-baked hills, carefully checking the area where the German student found his bones, but all we could find were a few more broken pieces. We then visited nearly every exposure of Triassic rock in the area, compass in hand and using our geological maps as our guides. All we seemed to find were a few little broken bones. There were no skeletons, not even anything we could identify as a dinosaur. We were very frustrated and about ready to quit.

On our final day, we returned to Penina to carefully retrace the steps of the German student. It was a brutally hot day, with the thermometers on our compasses reaching 120 degrees Fahrenheit (50 degrees Celsius)! We split up to maximize our chances of finding fossils. I stayed near the base of the hills, while Octávio and Richard climbed higher. A few minutes later I heard an excited scream from up on the ridge. Then, as quickly as it had started, the voice went quiet. Maybe the heat was playing with my mind and making me hear things? Just to be sure, I tried to follow the voice.

That's when I saw Octávio. When he saw me, he burst into song: 'I found it, I found it, I found it,' he repeated over and over. He was holding a bone.

Octávio showed Richard and me a 15-inch- (40-cm-) layer of mudstone rock, with many bones sticking out of it. The bones were packed together like toys in a toy box. Some bones were long and thick, others were broad and flat. Some looked like pieces of skulls, whereas others were clearly backbones or parts of limbs. The bones seemed to stick out at random angles. It looked like one big mess. And that's because it was. Octávio didn't just find one skeleton, he found a graveyard. There were hundreds, maybe even thousands, of skeletons packed together in this one layer of rock! It is the type of discovery that all paleontologists dream of.

WHAT HAPPENS ON A FOSSIL DIG

We returned to the Penina site over the next few years to carefully dig out the bones. We would usually go for one or two weeks at a time, in teams of about ten people. When we arrived, we would begin by setting up a large tarp on tall poles, to provide shelter from the hot sun. We would then use shovels and pickaxes to remove the dirt covering the bone layer, and the solid rock above the bone layer. Once we got down to the bone layer, we would take out smaller tools: hammers and chisels to remove the rock surrounding the bones, brushes to sweep away the dust to make sure we could see the bones, and tiny, sharp tools we got from dentists in order to remove small flakes of rock from the bone surface.

It would usually take many hours to expose a single bone from the rock. But at this point, we wouldn't yet remove the bones. They were too fragile and might break. We would first glue together any pieces of the bones that fell off, and then spray the bones with consolidant: a type of liquid plastic that hardens into a solid coat when it dries on the bones. Because it was so hot, it didn't take long for the consolidant to dry!

Paleontologist Steve Brusatte in Portugal with a supersalamander fossil in a plaster (consolidant) jacket.

Once the bones were dry, we would cover them up with newspaper. Then we would make a protective case for the bones out of plaster of paris, the same material doctors use to make casts to protect broken bones in humans. We would wrap bandages of wet plaster over the bones, wait for them to dry, and then when the 'plaster jacket' was hard, we would use hammers and chisels to separate it from the surrounding rock.

We did this, time and time again, for all the bones we were finding. Then we put all the plaster jackets into our vehicles and drove them to Octávio's lab. The hard plaster cast helped protect the fossils as we drove over bumpy roads. When we got back to the lab, Octávio sawed the plaster open, exposing the bones inside. He and his students could then use very fine tools to carefully remove each speck of dirt and rock from the bones, within the safety of the lab. This work – called *fossil preparation* – took a long time and a lot of patience, but at the end, the bones were completely freed from the rock. Then they could be studied and displayed in Octávio's museum.

If you were a small Triassic dinosaur, you would want to stay as far away from the water as possible. It was enemy territory. The supersalamanders were there waiting, ready to attack anything that ventured too close to the water. Their heads were the size of tables, and their jaws were hinged together at the back and could snap shut to gobble up whatever they wanted. It would only take a few bites to finish off a delicious dinosaur supper.

What animals dominated the land and where were they located?

With all the danger at the water's edge, maybe dry land was a safer place for the Triassic dinosaurs. But think again. The land was ruled by other enemies, which the dinosaurs needed to avoid. Some of the best fossils of these animals have been discovered by teams of young paleontologists. These fossils have been found through-out the southwestern United States, particularly New Mexico and Arizona.

Much of this area looks empty, with no buildings and few roads. You might walk all day without seeing another person. But the landscapes are very pretty. This type of landscape is called the 'badlands': a dry, colour-ful, rocky environment of hills, canyons, and strange natural rock shapes sculpted by the wind. Not much can grow here, and the area was very difficult to travel across in the days before cars. Because there is a lot of rock, the wind is constantly eroding it to expose new fossils, and there are no cities or plants to cover them up. It's a great place to discover fossils!

Much of the badlands in New Mexico and Arizona are made out of sandstone and mudstone rocks called the Chinle Formation, which formed in the ancient sand dunes and desert oases near the equator of Pangea from about 225 to 200 million years ago. Some of the best rocks can be found near the tiny town of Abiquiú, New Mexico, where only a few hundred people live. Beginning in the late 1800s, explorers began to find fossils in this area, and ever since, people have continued to discover thousands of fossils.

For many years now, a team of young researchers has worked near Abiquiú, and their discoveries are astonishing. At one site, called the Hayden Quarry, they found thousands of bones, which were buried by a flood about 212 million years ago. Because all these bones were buried together, they provide a picture of the ecosystem during that time.

Surprisingly, this was not an ecosystem dominated by dinosaurs. There were indeed some dinosaurs there, but not many, and none were particularly big or scary. All of them were meat-eating theropods. There is a human-sized hunter called *Tawa*, another similar-sized meat-eater that doesn't yet have a name, and a somewhat larger and stockier species called *Chindesaurus*. Each of these is represented by only a few fossils. These dinosaurs were very rare.

But other animals are much more common. There are some large amphibians similar to the supersalamanders we found in Portugal, and even little reptiles that hung from the trees like chameleons, called drepano-saurs.

The real superstars, however, were the crocs. Recall from the first chapter that dinosaurs are one side of the archosaur family tree. The other branch is made up of crocodiles and their extinct relatives, a group that I'll call the *crocs*. Many different types of crocs are found in the Hayden Quarry, and it was these creatures, not the dinosaurs, that dominated the land during the Triassic.

What were these crocs like? Forget everything you know about modern crocodiles. Yes, today's crocodiles and alligators can be frightening. They are strong, have sharp teeth, and sometimes attack humans. But there are only about twenty-five different species, they all pretty much look the same, and they can only live in hot areas near the equator.

The Triassic crocs were very different. They were diverse: there were many species, probably thousands. They were abundant: there were lots of them in each ecosystem. They lived all around the world. They had many diets, sizes, and behaviors. Some of them were nearly as big as buses, while others could fit in the palm of your hand. Some ate meat, some ate plants, some even lost their teeth entirely and had beaks. Most walked on all fours, but some only moved around on their hind legs, freeing up their arms to catch prey.

Among these Triassic crocs were species with long snouts that lived near the coasts. Others were plant-eaters with armour covering their bodies and spikes sticking out from their necks. Then there were the raui-suchians, a fierce group of meat-eaters.

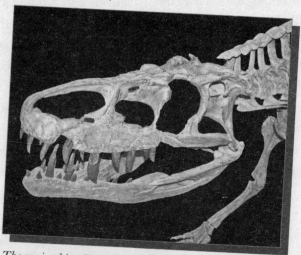

The rauisuchian Batrachotomus

If you want to envision a rauisuchian, imagine a slightly smaller version of a *T. rex* walking around on four legs, with a muscular skull, thick teeth, and a bone-breaking bite. The rauisuchians were on the top of the food chain during the Triassic. The dinosaurs, along with all other animals of the time, would have been ter-rified of them!

Why were dinosaurs lagging behind?

So the story is now very clear: dinosaurs existed during the Triassic Period, but they were not very important animals. They were not big, they were not common, and they were often food for other animals. This then raises a question: Why did it take so long for dinosaurs to become dominant?

To answer this question, we need to understand the environment these dinosaurs lived in. We need to look very closely at the rocks their fossils are found in, as these rocks contain many secrets.

JESSICA THE GEOLOGIST

Jessica Whiteside

Geologists are scientists who study the Earth. They want to know what the Earth is made of, how it has changed over time, and how it is changing today. Geologists love to study rocks because rocks provide clues about the environments, climates, and landscapes during the times they were formed.

In Portugal, I was fortunate to work with Jessica Whiteside, an amazing geologist, who is an expert at using rocks to understand past environments. She is such a good geologist that many paleontologists around the world ask her to work with them. She is also a key member of the team that studied the Hayden Quarry in New Mexico.

Jessica is a master at reading rocks. Better than anyone I've ever known, she can look at a series of rock layers and tell you how old they are, what the environments were like when they formed, how hot it was, even how much rain there was. Set her loose at a fossil site and she'll come back with a story from the distant past, of changing climates, shifting weather, and great extinctions.

How does Jessica do it? She looks very carefully at the rocks and determines what they are made of, which tells her where they formed. For example, sandstones often form on beaches or in river channels. She also looks at how the rocks are layered. Thin, straight layers might mean the rocks were laid down in a peaceful environment, but layers that cut across each other are a sign of fierce wind or water currents. She will do chemical analyses of the rocks, because different percentages of carbon and oxygen can be

formed only at certain temperatures or with a
certain amount of rainfall. By following all these
clues, Jessica can imagine what the world was
like when the rocks – and the fossils inside – were
made.

The geologist Jessica Whiteside has travelled the world
and visited many places where Triassic dinosaur bones
are found. She noticed a strange pattern. Dinosaurs
were rare all over the world during the Triassic, but
they do seem to be more common in some places
compared to others. In Argentina, for example,
there are many species of meat-eating and plant-
eating dinosaurs. But in New Mexico there are only three
types of meat-eaters, all of which are very similar to each
other. And in Portugal, where the supersalamanders
ruled, we have yet to find any dinosaurs at all.

All three places have different environments. The
New Mexico dinosaurs lived in a part of Pangea that
was near the equator, which at the time was a very hot
desert. Temperatures were well into the hundreds (or
35+ degrees Celsius) all year long, and there was little rain. This was a very difficult place to live. Some
animals, like the supersalamanders and many crocs,
learned to cope with these environments, but dinosaurs,
it seems, were not very good at living in the deserts.
Only the meat-eaters could survive there.

On the other hand, the Argentine dinosaurs lived

in a part of Pangea that was far south of the equator. This area was cooler than the deserts, and much wetter and more humid. It was a much easier place to live, and dinosaurs thrived in this type of environment. Not only were there meat-eaters, but there were plant-eaters too. That's probably because there were many more plants growing there than in the deserts.

Crocs and giant amphibians, however, were much more adaptable animals, so they colonized much of the world while the dinosaurs were stuck where they were.

Thus, even some 20 to 30 million years after they had evolved, and after their first fossils show up in Argentina, dinosaurs were still having trouble with the weather. But things would soon change . . .

4

Dinosaurs Become Dominant

Scottish sauropod

TIMELINE: Early-Middle Jurassic

ca. 200–170 million years ago

During the middle part of the Triassic Period, when the first dinosaurs were living in Argentina, the Earth began to crack. The dinosaurs would not have noticed, because it was happening far underground. But the cracks continued for tens of millions of years, until they reached the surface. Then earthquakes shook the ground, volcanoes shot lava and dust into the sky, and many plants and animals started to die.

What was going on? The world was breaking apart. Literally. The supercontinent of Pangea was splitting into separate pieces. It's because of these breaks that we have different continents today.

PLATE TECTONICS

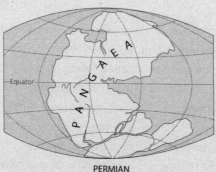

PERMIAN
250 million years ago

TRIASSIC
200 million years ago

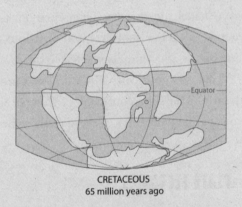

CRETACEOUS
65 million years ago

The break-up of Pangea in the Triassic was not that strange. Land is always moving, even now. This is a process called plate tectonics. The Earth's surface is divided into different regions, called plates, which can move over time. When two plates collide, mountains form. When two plates move apart from each other, lava comes up to fill the gaps, creating new land or seafloor.

And when two plates slide past each other, violent earthquakes can happen. This movement usually happens very slowly, about the same speed that our fingernails grow: an inch or so each year. It is powered by heat and pressure deep underground, which push and pull on the plates.

Today, parts of the Earth are breaking apart just as they did during the Triassic Period. For example, Africa is pulling away from the Middle East at the rate of about one centimeter per year. The two landmasses used to be connected about 35 million years ago, but now they are separated by the long and skinny Red Sea, which continues to get wider year by year and will one day turn into an ocean.

During most of the Triassic Period, forces from both the east and west were pulling on Pangea. The supercontinent began to stretch out and become thinner, until finally, at the very end of the Triassic Period, about 200 million years ago, the supercontinent began to break apart. North America separated from Europe. South America moved away from Africa – that's why even today these continents look like two pieces of a puzzle, because indeed they used to be connected! A little bit later, water would rush in to the fill the space between these new continents. But first, before the water, there was lava. Each crack in Pangea became a volcano.

The story was very similar to what happened more than 50 million years earlier, at the end of the Permian Period. Remember that the Permian ended with huge volcanic eruptions. The volcanoes released lava, but also poisonous gases that went into the atmosphere and warmed up the whole planet, killing many species. The same thing happened at the end of the Triassic. The volcanic gases caused global warming, which led to a mass extinction. Many plants and animals died out quickly, all over the world.

We can tell from the fossils that this would have been a bad time to be alive. If we compare fossils found in the rocks underneath the volcanic lava layers (animals that lived before the extinction) to fossils found in rocks above the lava (animals that lived afterward), the pattern is very clear: many species died. These species are common in the rocks underneath the lava, but are absent in the rocks above the lava.

Many of the animals that ruled the Triassic world went extinct. Almost all the crocs died. The only ones that survived were a few species, the ancestors of today's crocodiles and alligators. Most of the supersalamanders died too. Some smaller species survived, which is why today's salamanders are mostly tiny critters you can fit in your hand, not monsters the size of cars.

One group, however, survived. In fact, it seems like

the volcanoes and the global warming did not affect them at all. These animals were the dinosaurs!

The dinosaurs win

Somehow the dinosaurs were the winners. We just don't know why.

But what we do know is what happened afterward. The volcanoes stopped erupting. The climate cooled down. The surviving plants and animals – like the dinosaurs – had a new world in front of them. Gone were the fierce crocs and supersalamanders that dominated during the Triassic Period. With their competitors dead, the dinosaurs had a great opportunity to take over the world.

This was the start of the next period of time, the Jurassic Period, when dinosaurs became the huge, scary, amazing animals that we all know and love.

Over the first 30 million years of the Jurassic Period, dinosaurs evolved into many new species, including a variety of plant-eaters with beaks and big bellies. These were the ornithischian dinosaurs, the third major section of the dinosaur family tree, along with theropods and sauropodomorphs. Among the ornithischians were stegosaurs, which had plates on their backs and spikes on their tails, and ankylosaurs, whose bodies were covered with an armour-like coat of plates and spikes.

These Jurassic dinosaurs spread around the world,

hopping between the new continents that were continuing to move apart from each other. No longer were the dinosaurs restricted to certain areas. They now lived everywhere, even in the harsh deserts. These dinosaurs were also getting much bigger.

By the middle part of the Jurassic Period, about 170 million years ago, dinosaurs were truly dominant. They were the biggest, strongest, most important animals in ecosystems all over the planet. The image that we often see in books and movies had finally come to life: dinosaurs running across the land, at the top of the food chain, scary meat-eaters chasing huge long-necked sauropodomorphs and ornithischians, which tried to defend themselves with their plates and spikes and armor.

We now know so much about these dinosaurs that were evolving during the Jurassic Period because paleontologists today are finding more dinosaurs than ever before. Somebody, somewhere around the world, is discovering a totally new species of dinosaur every week! People are finding dinosaurs in places where scientists thought dinosaurs never existed. We're even finding dinosaurs in countries that might surprise you: like my new home of Scotland.

Scotland's Jurassic dinosaurs

Maybe you've seen television shows where paleontologists

dig up dinosaurs. A lot of these programs are the same. They show paleontologists – usually very muscular men wearing cowboy hats and jeans – who head into the desert, brave the heat, sweat a lot, find a dinosaur skeleton, and then brush sand off the bones. But this is misleading. Sometimes we do find dinosaurs this way, but usually paleontologists are everyday people who dress in many different types of clothing. Some are women, some are men. And we will go anywhere where there is rock that might contain dinosaur bones. Even Scotland.

Scotland is not a desert. It is not hot or dry. But it does have rocks that were formed during the Jurassic Period – rocks with dinosaur fossils inside. These rocks are found along the coast of a beautiful island called the Isle of Skye.

Today Skye is cold, windy, and rainy. The mountains are often covered in fog. It is a land of mystery. But during the Jurassic Period, it was much different. It was warmer, with a climate similar to that of Florida or the Mediterranean today. It was also part of an island back then, with tall mountains at the center. The mountains were drained by big rivers, which moved through thick jungles and along sparkling blue beaches, before emptying into the ocean. These environments were perfect for dinosaurs and for preserving rock, made from the sand and mud in the rivers and beaches. That's why we can find dinosaur fossils there today.

My favourite discovery is a vast tracksite of handprints and footprints of sauropod dinosaurs, which I made in 2015 with my friend paleontologist Tom Challands, at a place called Duntulm.

Paleontologists Steve Brusatte and Tom Challands in the Isle of Skye

THE ISLE OF SKYE

When I moved to Scotland in 2013, I became fascinated by the Isle of Skye. I read about the fossils discovered there. I was surprised that the first Skye dinosaur fossil – a single footprint – was discovered in the 1980s, around the time I was born. Since that time, people had discovered more footprints, but very few bones. Every once in a while, somebody would find a dinosaur tooth or a tailbone, but nobody had ever found a skeleton. That got me very excited. It seemed like there was opportunity to find more dinosaurs. All I had to do was look!

I didn't want to look alone, so I assembled a team. When I started my job at the University of Edinburgh, I quickly became friends with two other scientists. Tom Challands was a young paleontologist my age, and Mark Wilkinson was an experienced geologist. We decided to drive up to Skye together, where we met up with a local named Dugald Ross. Dugie, as he liked to be called, was not a scientist. He grew up on the Isle of Skye and makes a living farming and doing construction work. When he was a teenager, he discovered arrowheads and other artifacts left by ancient humans. He soon began to look for treasure all around his home island, including fossils. When he was nineteen years old, he built his own museum to display his discoveries. Today, his museum – the Staffin Museum – is very popular with tourists.

During that week, the four of us walked around the beaches and rock cliffs, picking up any fossils we found. We discovered a few bits and pieces: the jaw of a dog-sized crocodile, and the teeth and backbones of ichthyosaurs, strange reptiles that looked like fish and ruled the oceans when dinosaurs were living on the land. We didn't find any dinosaur fossils that time, but we returned to Skye many times over the next few years. Each time we reached the island, we hoped we would find a dinosaur. Finally, in the spring of 2015, we found what we were looking for, at Duntulm.

After a long day of fossil hunting, we were disappointed. We'd hoped to find dinosaur bones, but we had found nothing, and our patience was running out. We were cold and the tide was coming in, meaning that water would soon cover the rocky beach. And we were very hungry. So we packed up our gear and started to walk back to our cars.

That's when something caught our eye. Tom and I were walking together when we both saw a huge hole in the rock, about the size of a car tire.

'Look at this big thing!' Tom yelled to me. 'What do you think it is?'

As we continued to walk, we started to notice many other similar holes, which were now visible in the gentle early evening light. They were all about the same size, and the closer we looked, the more we saw that they stretched in every direction around us. They seemed to show a pattern. Individual holes were lined up in two long rows, in something of a zigzag arrangement. Left-right, left-right, left-right.

Tom and I both looked at each other. It was like we were reading each other's minds. We had seen these strange holes before, but not on the Isle of Skye – in other places we had gone to search for fossils.

'I know what they are!' I said to Tom, with a

big smile on my face.

The holes in front of us were handprints and footprints. Some of them even had finger and toe impressions. They were left by a massive animal that lived during the Jurassic Period. What type of animal? Well, there is really only one sort of animal that was so huge it left holes the size of car tires every time its hand or foot touched the ground.

'They're sauropod tracks,' I said to Tom, and he agreed.

A sauropod track found in the Isle of Skye.

Sauropods were the biggest dinosaurs ever. They evolved from smaller sauropodomorph ancestors that lived during the Triassic Period, like *Eoraptor* and *Ingentia* from Argentina. The Triassic species were mostly small, although some like *Ingentia* got as big as two elephants. But during the Jurassic Period, sauropods got even bigger. After the volcanoes killed the crocs and supersalamanders, the sauropods grew to monstrous sizes. The sauropod that left its tracks on the Isle of Skye is probably a species called *Cetiosaurus*, which was about 50 feet (16 metres) long, weighed around 27 tons (the size of five elephants!), and had a neck that extended two or three storeys into the sky.

The Isle of Skye tracksite is a 170-million-year-old dinosaur dance floor! The handprints and footprints were records of one of the first truly giant sauropods to ever live. And this was just the first discovery of many. It seems like every time we visit the Isle of Skye, we discover new dinosaur tracksites. We've now started to make maps of the tracksites using new technology: drones!

DRONES AND DINOSAURS

Paige dePolo

Drones are small flying machines with cameras that you can operate with a remote control. My student Paige dePolo is a master at using drones to study dinosaur tracksites. Paige studied geology and engineering in college, and then came to Edinburgh to do a master's degree. Her project combined two of her interests: dinosaurs and technology.

Paige brought her drone to each tracksite. She had to wait until the wind was calm before flying – which required a lot of patience on the cold and windy Isle of Skye! Once the drone was in the air, Paige used the remote control to move it back and forth over the tracksite. Usually the drone flew between 3 and 20 feet above the tracks. Paige programmed the drone to take a high-resolution photograph every few seconds. At the end of each flight, she would have hundreds or thousands of photographs. She then used software to stitch the photos together and create very detailed, three-dimensional computer maps of the tracksite. These maps help us understand how the tracksites were made, and what the dinosaurs that formed the tracks looked like.

These maps tell us many important things. First, lots of different dinosaurs left tracks on the Isle of Skye. Along with the sauropod tracks, there were also tracks made by both small (human-sized) and large (jeep-sized) meat-eating theropods, stegosaurs with plates on their backs, and a new type of dinosaur we haven't met yet: a duck-billed, plant-eating ornithischian.

Second, these tracks are often organized into track-ways: series of handprints and footprints made by an animal as it moved. Based on the spaces between the tracks, we can calculate the speed the dinosaurs were moving. Greater space between tracks equals greater speed. When we do these calculations for the Skye dinosaurs, we can tell that they were simply walking around. They weren't running, jumping, or chasing each other. It seems like they were just hanging around, living their lives. That means that these tracksites are like a window into history. They give us a glimpse into a random day in the lives of these dinosaurs.

Third, we can study the maps alongside the rocks the tracks are found in. This tells us something very interesting. Many of the tracks, including the sauropod handprints and footprints at Duntulm, were made by animals walking in shallow water. These dinosaurs were moving through a lagoon: a shallow body of water next to the beach. This is a strange image: dinosaurs much bigger than elephants, their necks stretched high into the air, stomping through the water!

PRESERVING DINOSAUR TRACKS

You might be wondering: How did the dinosaur tracks on the Isle of Skye survive for so long? If you've ever made footprints on a beach, you've probably seen them washed away by the next wave. The same thing would happen to most dinosaur tracks. But every once in a while, a storm might wash a layer of sand or mud over the dinosaur tracks, covering them up and protecting them. That's how the sauropod tracks at Duntulm were able to last for 170 million years!

It takes a lot of luck to form fossils and keep them preserved for millions of years. What are the odds that a thin layer of mud protects dinosaur footprints on a beach, or an avalanche of sand covers a dinosaur skeleton and turns it into stone? The chances are not good. Many trillions of animals have probably lived on the Earth over time, but very, very few have been turned into fossils. That is why paleontologists are so excited about fossils, and treat each one like a rare, delicate clue that must be protected and studied.

When we put the puzzle together, the Isle of Skye track-sites tell us that by the middle part of the Jurassic Period, dinosaurs had already taken over the world. There were many different types of dinosaurs – some big, some small; some that ate meat; others that ate plants; some with long necks, others sharp teeth, and others plates and spines on their back. These dinosaurs were living all over the world, and they were not only living on the dry land, but even in strange environments like lagoons.

There was no doubt about it: in the Jurassic Period, the dinosaurs had become spectacular.

5

Dinosaurs and Drifting Continents

Stegosaurus

TIMELINE: Middle–Late Jurassic

ca. 170–145 million years ago

Sauropods, like the ones that left their footprints on the Isle of Skye, were awesome animals. There is nothing alive today that looks anything like a long-necked, tiny-headed, big-bellied sauropod, or is anywhere near as big as a sauropod.

If somebody handed me a blank sheet of paper and a pencil and told me to create an imaginary beast, I doubt I could think of anything more incredible than a sauropod.

But we have to remember: sauropods were *real* animals. They were not creatures from myths or legends or made-up stories. They actually lived. They hatched from eggs. They grew from baseball-sized babies into adults larger than airplanes. They moved around on their thick arms and legs. They used their long necks to reach into the trees to eat. In fact, they ate lots of plants – probably more than 45 kilograms of leaves and stems every single day! They breathed air with their lungs, smelled with their noses, saw the world through their eyes.

Sauropods were the biggest animals that have ever lived on land in the entire 4.5-billion-year history of the Earth. The most gigantic sauropods, called titanosaurs, were more than 100 feet (31 metres) long from head to tail. Their necks could peer into a third- or fourth-floor window, if buildings had existed millions of years ago. They weighed more than 70 tons. In comparison, a Boeing 737 airplane (a common type of passenger plane that can carry about 200 people) weighs about 40 tons. So yes, I am serious when I say that some sauropods were bigger than airplanes!

The discovery of giants

The first scientists to discover and study sauropod bones in the 1820s were confused. They had no idea what type of ancient animal could have such large bones. So they guessed that the bones must have belonged to the only animals they knew could get so big: whales. It took a few decades, and many new discoveries, to reveal the truth. These bones did not belong to whales, but to a group of prehistoric reptiles with tiny heads, long necks, fat bellies, muscular legs, and long tails. These animals ate plants and literally caused small earthquakes every time they walked.

The first sauropod discoveries were isolated bones. A limb bone here, a back bone there, maybe a few teeth. But in the late 1800s, people started to find more complete skeletons. These people were railroad workers, cowboys, and other men looking to make some quick money. They were paid by scientists – Edward Cope and Othniel Marsh in particular (see below) – to explore the badlands, deserts, and mountains of western North America, particularly the states of Colorado, Utah, and Wyoming. They were instructed to go find as many bones as they could. Big dinosaurs or new species would earn more money.

THE BONE WARS

Edward Drinker Cope, the Bone Wars protagonist

Cope's Bone Wars rival, Othniel Charles Marsh (center, back row), and his team of student volunteers on their 1872 expedition to the American West

Edward Drinker Cope and Othniel Charles Marsh were wealthy, well-educated paleontologists who worked in big cities on the East Coast of the USA during the mid–late 1800s. Cope was based in Philadelphia, and Marsh at Yale University in Connecticut. They are two of the most famous dinosaur hunters who ever lived, not only because of their discoveries but because they fought each other for decades.

Cope and Marsh were once friends, but over time they became rivals, and then enemies. Each man wanted to prove that he was better and smarter than the other. But neither man wanted to spend too much time digging up dinosaur bones himself. After all, the mid–late 1800s was a violent time in the American West. The land had once belonged to the Native Americans, but it was being taken from them, one battle at a time. So instead, Cope and Marsh usually paid other people to do the hard work.

Cope and Marsh treated paleontology like it was a war. Their teams were made up of men, many of whom carried guns and liked to fight. They collected fossils as quickly as they could. They broke some fossils and mixed up others, so it was impossible to tell whether the bones they collected were from the same dinosaur or not. When one team couldn't find enough of their own fossils, they would sometimes steal from the other team. Other times they would intentionally destroy or break the other team's fossils. Some-times, one of the gun-carrying dinosaur hunters would get upset with Cope or Marsh, usually because they didn't pay enough money. So the dinosaur hunter would change sides and start working for the other team.

Today, we call this rivalry between Cope and Marsh the 'Bone Wars'. Obviously, this was not a good way to work and NOT how paleontologists dig up dinosaurs today. We carefully dig up dinosaurs using the 'plaster jacket' method that I described a couple of chapters ago. We take detailed notes and photographs, so we know where each fossil comes from and which bones belong together. Today's paleontologists have learned from the many mistakes of the Bone Wars.

And the explorers did find a lot of dinosaurs! That's because the western USA is full of dinosaur bones. All across this land, there is a thick unit of rock called the Morrison Formation. This rock can be found in thirteen different states, and covers nearly 400,000 square miles (1 million square kilometres). It formed during the latest part of the Jurassic Period, from around 156 to 146 million years ago. Back then, there was a range of tall mountains to the west. Rivers and streams carried water down from the mountains into swamps. Many dinosaurs lived in the jungles near the swamps and on the flat plains on the sides of the rivers. When the rivers flooded, they would bury dinosaur skeletons and turn them into fossils.

Many famous dinosaurs were first found by Cope's

and Marsh's teams during the 'Bone Wars' time. Among these are the large meat-eater *Allosaurus*, the horned meat-eater *Ceratosaurus*, and the plate-backed plant-eater *Stegosaurus*.

74

Stegosaurus, *one of the most famous dinosaurs discovered in the Morrison Formation during the Bone Wars period*

And then there were lots of sauropods. Have you ever heard of *Apatosaurus*, *Brontosaurus*, or *Diplodocus*? These well-known sauropods were also first discovered during the Bone Wars, as were *Barosaurus* and *Camarasaurus*. Then, after the Bone Wars ended, other paleontologists continued to find new sauropods in the Morrison rocks. *Brachiosaurus*, *Galeamopus*, *Kaatedocus*, *Dyslocosaurus*, *Haplocanthosaurus*, and *Suuwassea*, to name a few.

Many sauropods, living together

There were many, many sauropods that are found

together in the Morrison rocks, which means that many of these species probably lived together. This should strike you as odd, because in today's world, many large plant-eaters do not normally live together. But back in the Jurassic Period, numerous species of enormous sauropods were somehow able to survive side by side.

How did they do it? Although there were many species of sauropods, they were not all the same. Some were absolute giants, but others were smaller: *Brachiosaurus* was around 55 tons, *Brontosaurus* and *Apatosaurus* between 30 and 40 tons, and *Diplodocus* and *Barosaurus* were only 10 to 15 tons. So, some sauropods would need more food than others.

These sauropods also had different types of necks. The neck of *Brachiosaurus* stretched high into the sky, like a giraffe's. It could munch on the highest leaves in the treetops. *Diplodocus*, however, probably could not extend its neck much past its shoulders. It probably used its neck like a vacuum cleaner, to suck up shorter trees and bushes.

Finally, these sauropods had different types of heads and teeth. *Brachiosaurus* and *Camarasaurus* had deep, muscular skulls and broad teeth, so they could eat harder foods like thick stems and branches. But *Diplodocus* had a long head made up of thin bones, with a row of tiny pencil-shaped teeth at the front of its mouth. It would break its teeth if it tried to eat anything too hard.

Instead, it probably grabbed smaller leaves.

The diversity of these sauropods was key to their success. There were different species specialized for eating many different types of foods. They weren't competing for the same plants, but dividing the plants between them. The plants back then were different from today. There were no flowers or grasses, but there were lots of ferns and evergreen trees. These would have provided enough food for the many sauropods living together.

Why so big?

We now know why so many sauropods were able to live together. But there is an even greater mystery about sauropods. Why were they able to get so big?

It turns out that they had bodies that were perfectly suited for becoming big. There was not one single thing that made them able to grow to large sizes, but many factors working together.

To start, we need to think about what animals need in order to become really big.

First, they need a lot of food.

Second, they need to grow fast. If you grow slowly, over hundreds of years, maybe you will become big. But that is a lot of time for a predator to eat you, a disease to make you sick, or even for things like lightning strikes or floods to kill you.

Third, big animals need to have powerful lungs to take in a lot of oxygen. That's because they need more oxygen than smaller animals.

Fourth, they need to be built in a way that their skeleton is strong and sturdy, but not so heavy that it can't move.

And finally, really big animals need a way to stay cool. If they get too hot, they might get sick or die.

Sauropods must have been able to do all these things. And it all starts with the neck. The long, skinny neck is probably the most distinctive feature of sauropods. It allowed sauropods to reach higher in the trees than other plant-eating animals, which allowed them to eat more.

Then there's the way they grew. Sauropods grew fast: they changed from babies into adults within only thirty or forty years.

Next, they had special lungs. Not only were their lungs large, but they had strange balloon-like structures called *air sacs* sticking out from them. These air sacs stored oxygen-rich air, which allowed sauropods to take in two lungfuls of oxygen with each breath. These air sacs also had another function: they extended into the bones, making much of the skeleton hollow and light. The air sacs also acted as an air-conditioning system, helping the sauropods cool down on hot days.

So sauropods were like a puzzle. Their necks, lungs,

air sacs, and fast growth rates were all important. If you removed one of these things, sauropods would not have been capable of getting so big. Over millions of years of evolution, these puzzle pieces evolved one by one. At the end, evolution had made an animal that could eat a lot of food, grow quickly, breathe lots of oxygen, easily move around with a light skeleton, and cool itself down. That animal was now able to grow to enormous sizes.

During the Jurassic, sauropods found themselves able to grow to sizes that no animals, before or after, have been able to do. They became monstrously huge, swept around the world, and became dominant in the most magnificent way. And they would remain so for another hundred million years.

6

Jurassic Park to Cretaceous World

Carcharodontosaurus

TIMELINE: Late Jurassic–Early Cretaceous

ca. 164–125 million years ago

To summarize our story so far: the dinosaurs started out small and humble during the Triassic Period, survived the great extinction at the end of the Triassic that killed off many of their competitors like the crocs and supersalamanders, and then finally during the Jurassic Period the dinosaurs began to thrive.

Also during the Jurassic, new dinosaur species evolved, including meat-eaters and plant-eaters. They spread around the world. Some, like the sauropods, grew to enormous sizes. Throughout the Jurassic time, dinosaurs continued to diversify. There were now many different species living in different environments, from the poles to the equator and everywhere in between. Everywhere they lived, different dinosaurs joined to form *ecosystems*: a community of species living together, interacting with their environment. And when species live together, some of them are going to be predators, and some will be prey.

Food chains

In nature, there is a food chain. Meat-eaters are at the top of the chain. They hunt the plant-eaters, which eat the plants at the base of the food chain. But some sauropods were airplane-sized – what animals could possibly chase down, kill, and eat something so big?

The answer: theropod dinosaurs, the group of meat-eaters that includes *T. rex* and *Velociraptor*, along with thousands of other species. Few theropods were probably strong enough to take down a huge sauropod by themselves. But many meat-eating dinosaurs hunted in packs. Sometimes they may have worked together to attack a full-grown adult sauropod, but most of the time they probably targeted younger or weaker sauropods. This is often what lions and other predators do today.

Let's imagine what it would be like if you were a theropod dinosaur living in western North America in the Late Jurassic Period, about 150 million years ago.

There were many sauropods to hunt. You would have your choice of *Brontosaurus, Diplodocus,* or *Brachiosaurus,* to name a few. These would have been hard to kill, and you would probably need to team up with other theropods to capture one. If you did, though, you would have enough food for many days, or even weeks.

Or you could go for something smaller. There were many plant-eating dinosaurs that you could chase down and catch all by yourself.

Some of these might have been tricky to eat, like *Stegosaurus* (which had sharp spikes on its tail) and *Gargoyleosaurus* (which was covered in armour). But there were easier options. The duck-billed ornithischian *Camptosaurus* and smaller leaf-munchers like *Dryosaurus* didn't have any armour or weapons to keep predators away. As long as you could run them down, they probably made a very easy supper.

With so many potential prey species living in the swamps and river valleys, it is no surprise that there were many meat-eating dinosaurs in the Jurassic. Some of these were small, about the size of a dog. Others got bigger, up to the sizes of horses or large cars. And there was one species that got very big, about the size of a school bus. This was *Allosaurus*, one of the first truly ferocious giant flesh-eating dinosaurs that ever lived.

83

ALLOSAURUS: THE BUTCHER OF THE JURASSIC

The first fossils of *Allosaurus* were discovered during the Bone Wars. *Allosaurus* was described as a new species by Othniel Charles Marsh in 1877. He didn't realize it at the time, but *Allosaurus* would become a famous dinosaur. After the Bone Wars ended, the science of paleontology began to change. Many new groups of scientists went out to the western United States to look for dinosaurs, but they didn't fight each other and steal fossils. By paying more attention to actually finding dinosaur bones rather than beating their rivals, these teams made many amazing discoveries.

One of the most important new finds was the Cleveland-Lloyd Dinosaur Quarry, near the small town of Price, Utah, which contains more than 10,000 dinosaur bones. Most of the bones found here belong to *Allosaurus*. It seems that about fifty different *Allosaurus* skeletons are mixed together, and these fossils have allowed paleontologists to study *Allosaurus* in detail, which means it is now one of the best understood dinosaurs of all.

Allosaurus was the Butcher of the Jurassic. It was a distant cousin of *T. rex*, which also lived in western North America, but about 80 to 90 million years later. *Allosaurus* looked like *T. rex*, but was a little smaller and lighter. Like *T. rex*, it had a large head with sharp teeth, small arms with sharp claws, and a long tail for balance. It walked only on its hind legs. An adult *Allosaurus* was about 30 feet (9 metres) long and weighed between 2 and 2.5 tons. That is indeed smaller than *T. rex* (which was about 40 feet (12 to 13 metres) long and 7 to 8 tons), but this gave *Allosaurus* an advantage: it was faster and more agile, so it could chase down prey easier.

But that's not the most terrifying thing about *Allosaurus*! There is a reason scientists nickname it the Butcher. We think it actually used its head like a giant axe to hack into its prey, kind of like a butcher using a big cleaver knife to cut up steaks. We know that *Allosaurus* could open its jaws very wide, and computer models tell us that its skull bones were very strong. So we think a hungry *Allosaurus* would attack with its mouth open and slash down at its prey, slicing through skin and muscle with its sharp teeth. Although it is a bloody scene to imagine, many a *Brontosaurus*, *Stegosaurus*, and *Camptosaurus* probably met their end in this way.

The Jurassic world

Allosaurus ruled the Jurassic. It lived in North America as well as Europe and maybe even in Africa too. Although the continents were continuing to move apart, there were still connections between much of the world. North America, Europe, and Asia were separated by water, but there were islands between them. Dinosaurs could have hopped along these islands to migrate.

The southern continents, however, were still mostly joined together into a landmass called Gondwana. South America, Africa, Australia, and Antarctica were united, with small cracks starting to separate them. India was also part of this southern giant continent – many millions of years later, it would begin moving north, and then collide with Asia to form the Himalayan mountains.

The main separation in the Jurassic globe was between north and south. There was an ocean separating the northern lands (North America, Europe, and Asia) from Gondwana. But this seaway too had islands that dinosaurs could move across. As you can see, it wouldn't have been too difficult for *Allosaurus*, or any other dinosaur, to wander around the Jurassic world.

Into the Cretaceous

The Jurassic time period could not last forever. About 145 million years ago, it ended and the next period began: the Cretaceous. This was a calm transition. Remember that when the Triassic Period changed into the Jurassic Period, the supercontinent began to split, volcanoes erupted, and many species died. But there was no similar catastrophe as the Jurassic turned into the Cretaceous. Instead, the changes between the Jurassic and Cretaceous were milder. The continents continued to separate, climates switched from hot to cold and back again, and sea levels slowly fell, exposing more island and land bridges that allowed dinosaurs to migrate around the world. None of these changes were fast, though (they took about 20 million years!), and none were deadly on their own. But added together, they did cause the dinosaurs to evolve.

By about 125 million years ago, 20 million years after the Jurassic ended, a new Cretaceous world had emerged. Very different dinosaurs now ruled the land.

The most obvious change had to do with the most prominent dinosaurs: those long-necked, big-bellied sauropods. In the Jurassic there were so many sauropods, living together, feeding on different types of plants.

In the Cretaceous, however, the sauropods declined. They did not die out, but they changed. There were fewer species, but some of them became even larger than their Jurassic cousins.

The age of the titanosaurs

The titanosaurs were sauropods that got bigger than airplanes. Some of the most famous titanosaurs are *Argentinosaurus*, *Dreadnoughtus*, and *Patagotitan*. Still, even though these titanosaurs became huge, many other types of sauropods disappeared.

As the sauropods suffered, smaller plant-eating ornithischians took their place. Duck-billed species like *Iguanodon* and armour-covered ankylosaurs became the main plant-eaters in many ecosystems.

The meat-eating dinosaurs also changed dramatically. Many new species of small carnivores appeared, including smart, feisty, claw-footed 'raptors' of the *Velociraptor* family, which we will learn about more in later chapters. Some of these new theropods started to do strange things. They stopped eating only meat and started to feast on new foods, like nuts, seeds, bugs, and shellfish. One group, the big-bellied and big-clawed therizinosaurs, even became vegetarians! Another group, the huge spinosaurs – with long skulls, thick legs, and sails on their backs – moved into the water and started to eat fish.

We don't know exactly why the theropods started eating new foods, but it is probably because new types of plants and fish were evolving, so the theropods took advantage of the opportunity to expand their diets.

My favorite theropods, however, are the apex predators. They are at the very top of the food chain – the biggest and most dominant meat-eaters of all. In the Jurassic, *Allosaurus* was king. But *Allosaurus* went extinct, although we don't know why. It was then replaced by a new type of huge carnivore in the Cretaceous: the carcharodontosaurs.

The carcharodontosaurs were the first dinosaurs I studied when I trained to become a paleontologist in college.

MY FIRST DINOSAUR

I was born and raised in the Midwestern United States, in a small farming town in northern Illinois. In many ways I was a normal teenager. I watched movies and listened to music and went to baseball games. But I was also obsessed with dinosaurs. My hero was not an athlete or an actor. He was paleontologist Paul Sereno, who travelled the world digging up dinosaurs and taught at the University of Chicago, about an hour and a half from my home. He also grew up in Illinois, and then became a famous dinosaur hunter. I wanted to be like him.

I met Paul when I was fifteen years old. He was lecturing at a local museum. I was very nervous, but I went up to talk to him after his lecture was over. He showed me some of the dinosaur fossils he'd brought along. He told me to keep in touch, and encouraged me to study at the University of Chicago after I finished high school. A few years later, I did just that.

During my first week of college in 2002, I met Paul in his laboratory. All around me were dinosaur bones. Some were put together into a complete skeleton display, like you would see in a museum. Others were still inside rock, and Paul's team was using saws, drills, and other tools to carefully remove them. Many of these dinosaurs were from Africa and China, places that Paul regularly went to look for new fossils.

I hoped that maybe one day, I could join Paul on one of his adventures. But first I would need to learn a lot. Over the next year, Paul taught me how to identify fossils, catalogue and photograph them, use small drills to clean away the rock. He showed me how to use clay and plastic to make perfect copies of fossils. He taught me the names of the different bones, and how they fit together to make a skeleton.

Then, one day, Paul led me to a row of cabinets, each one full of new dinosaur bones he had yet to study.

'How would you like to describe a new dinosaur?' he asked me while he opened a drawer.

Spread in front of me, drawer after drawer, were fossils of dinosaurs that Paul and his team had recently brought back from the Sahara Desert in Africa. These dinosaurs lived during the early and middle parts of the Cretaceous Period, during the time that sauropods were declining and after carcharodontosaurs had replaced *Allosaurus* at the top predators.

I didn't know very much about African dinosaurs. It turns out, not many other people did either. People have been finding and studying dinosaur bones in North America and Europe for two centuries, but much less work has been done in Africa. This was the terrible result of colonialism. During the late nineteenth and early twentieth centuries, European countries went to Africa, took the land, and controlled most of the continent. Some European explorers, however, went to countries like Tanzania, Niger, and Egypt, where they did discover some dinosaur bones. These fossils were taken back to Europe. But then, many of the dinosaur bones were destroyed during World War II.

Paul became interested in African dinosaurs in the 1990s, and began to work with scientists in Morocco and Niger. Together, they went into the desert, and over many years, they found many dinosaurs. They discovered so many skeletons that Paul needed to rent a warehouse to store them all! One of their greatest discoveries was the bathtub-sized skull of a giant flesh-eater called

Carcharodontosaurus saharicus, in Morocco. This was the best fossil of a carcharodontosaur that had yet been discovered. And it was a real glimpse at the big meat-eaters that took over from *Allosaurus* and became the biggest, fiercest, meanest predators of the Cretaceous.

As my eyes scanned the drawers in front of me, Paul stopped and picked up a bone, part of the face of an enormous meat-eating dinosaur. There were other bones in the same drawer: a piece of a lower jaw, some teeth, and the fused bones from the back of the head that would have surrounded the brain and ears. Paul told me how he'd discovered the fossils a few years earlier in an empty part of Niger called Iguidi, just west of a desert oasis. It was hot, dry, and dusty. The bones were found in a red sandstone, which was formed in a river between 95 and 100 million years ago, when this part of Africa was much different. It was warm, wet, and humid, with jungles, lakes, beaches, and rivers that were full of dinosaurs and other life.

Paul handed me the huge face bone. 'It looks really similar to the *Carcharodontosaurus saharicus* bones I found in Morocco,' he told me as he pointed out the deep holes that had once held long knife-blade teeth. 'But there also are some differences. Maybe it is a new species.'

I stared up at Paul, not sure what to say next. He then broke the silence.

'I want you to figure it out!' he said to me.

'Spend the summer here, study the bones, and tell me what you think.'

When Paul Sereno gave me the dinosaur bones to study, I had one main goal: to determine whether the bones belonged to a dinosaur that had already been found, or whether they were from a totally new species.

I began by taking all the bones, putting them out on a table, and looking at them for days. I held them in my hands. I observed what features they had. How many teeth were in the jawbones. The shape of the suture line where two of the skull bones connected. The positions of holes for nerves and blood vessels in the bones around the brain. And so on. I made many notes and drawings, and I took careful measurements and photographs of all the bones.

During this time, I had many textbooks and reports open in front of me. I needed to make sure that I was identifying each bone and each feature correctly. The best way to do that was to read what other scientists had written about other dinosaurs and follow what they had done.

After I had spent a lot of time looking at the bones, it was time to compare them to the bones of other dinosaurs. This is how we really know whether or not we have a new species. Each dinosaur species is defined by its own unique set of characteristics. If you find a skeleton that has all the characteristic features of, say, *Carcharodontosaurus saharicus*, then that means your new skeleton is a *Carcharodontosaurus saharicus*. But if you find a skeleton with some unusual features not seen in any other dinosaurs, that means you have a new species. It sounds simple, but this work takes a lot of time. You need to carefully compare your dinosaur to all the other dinosaurs, and you need to do this one bone at a time.

After a few months of studying the bones from Niger, I concluded that the bones were very similar to the skull bones of *Carcharodontosaurus saharicus*, which Paul had found in Morocco. The bones were all very big. The bones of the face were covered in many pits and grooves. The teeth were long and thin, with many tiny serrations on their edges, like a knife. There were large, hollow sinuses inside the bones surrounding the brain. These are all signature features of *Carcharodontosaurus saharicus*.

Jawbone of a Carcharodontosaurus saharicus

On the other hand, the Niger fossils had some differences – mostly subtle things, which I only learned to recognize after looking at a lot of bones. They included a much smaller sinus in front of the eyes and a deeper muscle attachment on the side of the back of the skull.

So what did this mean? Clearly the Niger fossils were from an animal similar to *Carcharodontosaurus saharicus*, but not identical. The new bones had their own distinctive features, which means they must belong to a new species. Paul and I named this species *Carcharodontosaurus iguidensis*. It was the first dinosaur species I ever named, and it was an amazing feeling, to be the first person to identify a dinosaur that lived millions of years ago, which no humans have ever seen alive. Since that time, I've named another fifteen or so dinosaur species. But the first one will always be the most special.

When I was a student, I described a new species of carcharodontosaur, *Carcharodontosaurus iguidensis*. It was the top predator of the humid seaside ecosystems of middle Cretaceous Africa. It was about 40 feet long (12 to 13 metres) and weighed around 3 tons. It was bigger than *Allosaurus* from the Jurassic, and was about as long as the great *T. rex* itself (which was still many tens of millions of years in the future).

There was a whole group of dinosaurs like

Carcharodontosaurus iguidensis that lived across the world during the early and middle parts of the Cretaceous. These are the carcharodontosaurs. Other members of the group are *Giganotosaurus* from South America, *Acrocanthosaurus* from North America, *Concavenator* from Europe, and *Shaochilong* from Asia. This last dinosaur is a species that I also named, after finding the bones misidentified in a museum drawer in China.

These carcharodontosaurs were amazing dinosaurs. They got their start in the latest part of the Jurassic Period, and evolved from ancestors that were very similar to *Allosaurus* itself. So the carcharodontosaurs and *Allosaurus* were close cousins. When *Allosaurus* went extinct at the end of the Jurassic, the carcharodontosaurs survived and moved into the top predator role. They grew to even bigger sizes and could probably eat almost anything they wanted.

The South American species *Mapusaurus* has been found in a bonebed: a graveyard with at least seven skeletons. This suggests they lived in groups, and maybe even were pack hunters. If so, they could probably hunt sauropods. It is also probably not a coincidence that one of the largest sauropods of all, *Argentinosaurus*, lived alongside *Mapusaurus.* Perhaps some carcharodontosaurs became so big in order to hunt sauropods.

But as big and mean as these carcharodontosaurs were, they wouldn't stay on top forever. Living alongside them, in their shadow, was another breed of carnivore that was smaller, faster, and brainier. They are called the tyrannosaurs. And they would soon make their move and begin a whole new dinosaur empire.

7

The Tyrant Dinosaurs

Qianzhousaurus

TIMELINE: Middle Jurassic–latest Cretaceous
ca. 170–66 million years ago

T. *rex* is the most famous tyrannosaur. But many other meat-eating dinosaurs belong to the tyrannosaur group. Over the last fifteen years, paleontologists have discovered many new tyrannosaur species – about twenty in total. Many of these are much older and much smaller than *T. rex*, and they lived all around the world. These discoveries help us make a family tree of the tyrannosaurs, which tells the story of how evolution produced such a remarkable creature as *T. rex*.

Tyrannosaurus rex means 'tyrant lizard king', and it is a perfect name for this dinosaur. It was 40 feet long (12 to 13 metres) and weighed 7 or 8 tons.

Skull of a Tyrannosaurus rex

It bit so hard that it crushed the bones of its prey. As far as we know, it was the largest meat-eater to ever live on Earth. It lived about 66 to 67 million years ago, right at the end of the Cretaceous Period, and was one of the last dinosaurs that ever lived. It was there when a six-mile-wide asteroid hit the Earth, causing dinosaurs to go extinct. But we're getting ahead of ourselves. That part of our story will come later.

The first *T. rex* fossils were discovered in the early 1900s in the western United States (see below). Over the next few decades, paleontologists discovered other new dinosaurs that were similar to *T. rex*. There was *Albertosaurus* and *Gorgosaurus* from Canada, and *Tarbosaurus* from Asia. All these dinosaurs looked more or less the same – they were bus-sized, with huge heads, sharp teeth, and tiny arms. *T. rex* was the biggest, but the others were almost the same size. All these species lived in the very latest part of the Cretaceous Period, between about 84 and 66 million years ago. Different species lived at different times, and they were always the top predators in their ecosystems.

THE DISCOVERY OF *T. REX*

The first *T. rex* fossils were discovered by Barnum Brown. Brown grew up in a small town in Kansas and became interested in nature at a young age. He collected rocks and shells, and made a small museum to display them at his house.

When he got older, he moved to New York City and started collecting dinosaur bones for the American Museum of Natural History. Over time, he became one of the greatest dinosaur hunters who ever lived. He had some unusual behaviors: he searched for fossils in the summer while wearing a full-length

Barnum Brown

fur coat, and made extra money as a spy!

One day, in 1902, Brown was walking in the badlands of eastern Montana, near a little waterway called Hell Creek, and came across a jumble of bones. There was part of a skull and jaw, some backbones and ribs, bits of the shoulder and arm, and most of the pelvis. The bones were enormous: they belonged to an animal that was somewhere around 10 feet (3 metres) tall, stood on two legs, and had sharp teeth. It was much bigger than *Allosaurus*, which was the largest known predatory dinosaur at that time. Clearly this was a meat-eating dinosaur, but what was it?

Brown sent the bones to New York, where they were cleaned and studied. They were so big that it took a few years to assemble the bones into a skeleton, which was then put on display. The new dinosaur was named *Tyrannosaurus rex*, and it became a sensation. Crowds flocked to the museum, and it started to appear as a character in movies and books. Very quickly, *T. rex* became a famous dinosaur, as it remains today!

Where did these mighty, scary carnivores come from? How were they able to get so big? Until about fifteen years ago, we didn't know the answers to these questions. But now, because of all the new tyrannosaur fossils scientists have been discovering around the world, we do!

These new fossils tell us something very interesting and unexpected: tyrannosaurs are a very old group, which started about 170 million years ago. The first tyrannosaurs were small, not much bigger than humans. They stayed that way for most of their history, until the giant species appeared right at the end of the Age of Dinosaurs.

NEW TYRANNOSAUR DISCOVERIES

On a hot summer day in 2010, a construction worker in Ganzhou, China, was working a backhoe, digging up dirt and rock to clear space for a new office building. He raised the backhoe's bucket into the air, and then brought it down to the ground.

CRUNCH!

The construction worker stopped. The backhoe

must have hit something hard, maybe a pipe or an electrical line. As the dirt and smoke cleared, he did not see any damaged pipes or wires. Instead, he saw fossilized bones, lots of them, some of which were really huge.

The construction worker had discovered a new dinosaur completely by accident!

Government officials raced to the work site, put together a team, and collected all the bones. It took them six hours, and they filled twenty-five bags. They took the fossils to the town's museum, where scientists began to study the bones and put them back together. They were shocked. The bones joined into a nearly complete skeleton, which looked very similar to the skeleton of the famous *T. rex*. But it was smaller than *T. rex*, and its skull bones looked different.

The museum scientists needed the help of a dinosaur expert, so they called Junchang Lü, the legendary dinosaur hunter who we met at the beginning of this book.

Paleontologists Junchang Lü and Steve Brusatte where Qianzhousaurus was discovered

Junchang confirmed that the skeleton did belong to a tyrannosaur, the group of theropods that includes *T. rex* and its closest cousins. But Junchang wasn't sure what type of tyrannosaur it was, so he then asked me to help.

Junchang showed me some photos of the new discovery, and I thought the bones looked different from any tyrannosaur I had ever seen. But I would need to see the bones with my own eyes to be sure. So I went to China, met Junchang, and together we looked at each bone, took notes and photographs, and compared the bones to those of other tyrannosaurs. After this careful work, we concluded that the construction worker had indeed discovered a new species.

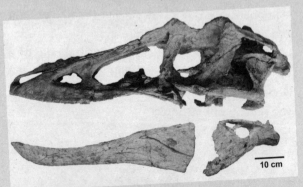

The skull of Qianzhousaurus

We named the new tyrannosaur *Qian-zhousaurus*, in reference to the part of China where it was found. This name is difficult to spell and pronounce, and even I don't get it correct sometimes. So we decided to give it a nickname,

'Pinocchio rex', because it had a very long nose. It also had small horns sticking up from its nose. These are the two main ways in which it differs from *T. rex*.

The discovery of *Qianzhousaurus* goes to show that not all tyrannosaurs looked exactly like *T. rex*. In fact, most of them did not look like *T. rex* at all!

The oldest, smallest tyrannosaurs

For the moment, we need to jump back in time, before the Cretaceous Period, and go back to the Jurassic, the age of long-necked sauropods and the Butcher *Allosaurus*. The oldest tyrannosaur we know about comes from the Jurassic. It is a species called *Kileskus*, found in the mosquito-filled forests of Siberia in northern Russia. It looks very different from the *T. rex* we all know. Only a handful of its bones have been discovered, but these are very small. *Kileskus* probably weighed only around 100 pounds (45 kilograms), and its skeleton was not much bigger than a human's!

Kileskus lived in the middle part of the Jurassic, around 170 million years ago, right around the same time sauropods were leaving their handprints and footprints in the lagoons of the Isle of Skye. This was more than

The finger bone of Kileskus

100 million years before *T. rex* lived!

While *Kileskus* is still only known from a few bones, there is another small tyrannosaur from later in the Jurassic that is easier to study. This is *Guanlong*, from China.

Skull of Guanlong, *with the crest of bone on the top of its head*

It weighed about 150 pounds (70 kilograms), and had long legs, a skinny body, and a long tail. It had sharp teeth and three fingers on its arms, each of which ended in a pointy claw. *Guanlong* also had a tall crest of bone on top of its head, which looks like a Mohawk haircut. The crest was probably used for display: to attract mates and scare away rivals.

There is no doubt that *Guanlong* was a good hunter. It could run fast on its slim legs, and catch prey with its sharp teeth and deadly claws. But *Guanlong* was not a top predator. It lived alongside much larger carnivores like *Sinraptor*, a 30-foot-long (9 metres) cousin of

Allosaurus that weighed more than a ton. At best *Guanlong* was a second- or third-tier predator, many links below the top predators on the food chain. The same was probably true of *Kileskus*, and many other recently discovered species of small tyrannosaurs that lived in the Jurassic and the early part of the Cretaceous.

But if *Guanlong* and *Kileskus* were so tiny, and looked so different from *T. rex*, why do we classify them as tyrannosaurs? They actually have many features in common. They all have fused nasal bones above their noses, a wide snout at the front of the jaws, a small horn in front of each eye, and two big bone ridges on the pelvis where strong leg muscles attached. No other theropods (like *Allosaurus* or carcharodontosaurs) possess these features, which means they are unique features that define the tyrannosaurs.

107

THE WORLD'S GREATEST DINOSAUR HUNTER

Xu Xing

The small tyrannosaur *Guanlong* was described in 2006 by the Chinese paleontologist Xu Xing and his colleagues. Xu and his team discovered two nearly complete skeletons of *Guanlong*, one an adult and the other a teenager.

Xu is the world's most decorated dinosaur hunter. He has named more dinosaurs than anyone else alive – more than 60 species. Scientists from around the world travel to China to work with Xu, and farmers and construction workers from across China often send Xu new fossils that they discover.

When Xu was young, he never imagined he would become a famous scientist. He grew up poor in Xinjiang, a large area of western China. Unlike many children in western countries, Xu had no interest in dinosaurs when he was in school. He didn't even know dinosaurs existed. But he then won an award that paid for his college education. In order to get the award, he was told he needed to study paleontology. He was confused: he had never heard of this subject before! But Xu said yes, and began his studies. He was a quick learner, and before long was discovering and naming dozens of new dinosaur species.

Tyrannosaurs become big

Tyrannosaurs started out small, and they stayed small during the Jurassic (the time of *Kileskus* and *Guanlong*) and then afterward for most of the Cretaceous. They lived all across North America, Asia, and Europe, and some scrappy fossils suggest they lived on the southern landmass of Gondwana too. These early tyrannosaurs were very good at being small-to-mid-sized predators living in the bushes. So why change?

To solve this mystery, we first need to see when larger tyrannosaurs appeared, species that look like *T. rex* and its very closest cousins. These tyrannosaurs were over 35 feet (11 metres) long and weighed more than 1.5 tons, and had big heads, muscular jaws, banana-sized teeth, tiny arms with only two claws, and bulky leg muscles. We find the first fossils of these giants in rocks from the Late Cretaceous Period that formed between 80 and 84 million years ago. The oldest big tyrannosaurs are found in western North America, and soon afterward they are found in Asia too. But they have never been found in Europe or the southern continents.

What this means is that the switch between small and big tyrannosaurs happened sometime in the middle part of the Cretaceous, between 85 and 110 million years ago. Before this time, almost all the tyrannosaurs were like *Kileskus* and *Guanlong*: human-sized, fast-running hunters living in the shadows of other giant dinosaurs. After this time, enormous tyrannosaurs like *T. rex* reigned. Unfortunately, very few fossils are found between 85 and 110 million years ago. This is a gap in the fossil record.

But a few years ago, we finally found a good clue. These new fossils are about 90 million years old, and come from another unexpected place: Uzbekistan, a vast country in central Asia (see below). They are a handful of bones from the skeleton of a horse-sized dinosaur, including part of a skull that my colleagues and I studied with a CAT scanner, a machine that uses X-rays to see inside fossils and other objects.

THE DISCOVERY OF *TIMURLENGIA*

The bones of the new tyrannosaur *Timurlengia* were discovered during an expedition led by the Russian paleontologist Alexander 'Sasha' Averianov (the same scientist who named *Kileskus*) and his German-American friend Hans-Dieter Sues. After they found these bones, they invited me to help study them.

Russian paleontologist Alexander 'Sasha' Averianov with Steve Brusatte

The invitation was a surprise. I was in St Petersburg, Russia, visiting Sasha to study the bones of *Kileskus*. It was a cold day in early spring, and the river outside was still full of ice. After I looked at *Kileskus*, Sasha handed me a small box. Inside was a braincase: a set of bones that fit together like a puzzle to surround the brain and ears.

'What do you think it is?' Sasha asked as I took the grapefruit-sized fossil in my hand.

I looked at it carefully for several minutes. The braincase looked very similar to another braincase I had studied recently, but it was much smaller.

'I might be wrong,' I told Sasha, 'but this looks like *T. rex*. It has all the same bones and nerve openings. But it is so small!'

Sasha smiled. 'That's what I thought too,' he said as he took the fossil from me, wrapped it in a cloth, and put it back in the box. 'We'll study it together.'

A few months later, after cleaning the fossil further, Sasha met me again and handed over the skull.

When I got back to Edinburgh, I unpacked the fossil and brought it to my colleague Ian Butler, a geologist and a chemist, and also a great builder of machines. He had built his own CAT scanner, and we used it to scan the fossil. My student Amy Muir then made a digital model of the brain and ear using special computer graphics software.

CAT SCANNERS

Computerized axial tomography (CAT) scanners are powerful machines that shoot X-rays to see inside objects. A computer can then take the X-rays, add them together using sophisticated software, and create a three-dimensional model. This is very useful for medical doctors. Let's say you go to the doctor with a pain in your stomach. It's too dangerous for a doctor to immediately cut into your stomach to see what is wrong. So first the doctor might put you in a CAT scanner and use the X-rays to see inside your stomach. By looking at the digital model of your stomach on their computer screen, the doctor can hopefully figure out what is wrong with you without needing to do surgery.

Paleontologists use CAT scanners for similar reasons. There is a lot of information hidden inside dinosaur skulls, like the brain, ear canals, and sinuses. We often want to know what these things looked like because they can tell us how smart dinosaurs were and what their senses were like. Many decades ago, paleontologists would sometimes cut open the skulls of dinosaurs with saws, to see these spaces. While this revealed a lot of information, it also caused a lot of damage. One skull of *T. rex* was nearly destroyed this way! Modern paleontologists now use CAT scanners, and this has revolutionized the science of paleontology. Today, paleontologists like me use CAT scanners all the time!

> > >

By CAT scanning the skull, we discovered something fascinating.

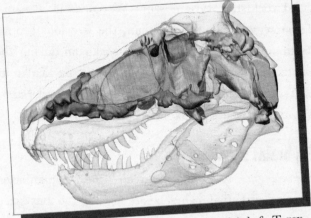

CAT scan of the head of a T. rex

First, the brain had the characteristic shape of a *T. rex* brain: it was long and tube-shaped, with many blood vessels near the back. This confirmed that the Uzbekistan fossil was a tyrannosaur.

Not only that, but the brain was very large for a horse-sized animal, meaning it was an intelligent creature. The same is true of *T. rex*: it had a large brain too.

Plus, we could see that the ear had a very long cochlea. The cochlea is the part of the ear that hears sounds, and we know from living animals that the longer the cochlea is, the wider range of sounds it can hear. The Uzbekistan tyrannosaur, just like *T. rex*, had a great sense of hearing.

In 2016, our team worked together to describe the Uzbekistan tyrannosaur. We gave it a name: *Timurlengia*, in honor of Timur, the ferocious central Asian warlord who ruled over Uzbekistan during the fourteenth century. *Timurlengia*, and in particular its CAT-scanned brain and ear, finally help us understand why tyrannosaurs got big.

Big brains survive

Timurlengia was in between the human-sized tyrannosaurs that came before it and the bus-sized monsters that came after it. It was living in an ecosystem that was still controlled by carcharodontosaurs, so it was not a top predator. But, while it was living lower down on the food chain, it was developing a larger brain, greater intelligence, and a keener sense of hearing. We don't know why, but maybe these were superpowers that helped it survive in a world controlled by carcharodontosaurs.

Then it seems like there was a period of environmental change. Temperatures got hotter, sea levels went up and down, and the oceans lost much of their oxygen. These things probably caused the top predators, like most carcharodontosaurs, to go extinct. Tyrannosaurs like *Timurlengia*, with their smaller bodies and big brains, survived. And then, afterward, these tyrannosaurs had a great opportunity. There were no apex, or top, predators anymore, so tyrannosaurs moved in and took the job.

Tyrannosaurs, therefore, became smart before they became big. Their brains probably helped them outsmart the top predators of the day, and then survive climate change in the middle Cretaceous. Then during the next 20 million years of the latest Cretaceous, huge tyrannosaurs like *T. rex* flourished. They ruled the river valleys, lakeshores, plains, forests, and deserts of North America and Asia. They were especially scary because they had both brains and brawn! Or in other words, they were smart and they were big.

The ultimate tyrannosaur – *the ultimate dinosaur* – was *T. rex* itself. Let me now tell you more about the King of the Dinosaurs.

8

The King of the Dinosaurs

Tyrannosaurus rex

TIMELINE: latest Cretaceous

ca. 67–66 million years ago

Almost everybody has heard of *T. rex*. It is surely the most famous dinosaur of all. But *T. rex* was not a monster. It was a real animal.

So what was *T. rex* like as a living, breathing, feeding, moving, growing animal? In this chapter, I will introduce you to the real *T. rex*. To do this, I will also introduce you to some of the scientists who are using cutting-edge research to understand what *T. rex* was like when it ruled North America during the very latest part of the Cretaceous Period, from about 67 to 66 million years ago.

Let's remember why *T. rex* was the King of the Dinosaurs.

T. rex

First, *T. rex* was huge. Adults were about 40 feet (12 to 13 meters) long, and weighed around 7 to 8 tons. That's bigger than any other purely meat-eating dinosaur that we know of. In fact, *T. rex* is the biggest carnivore—*of any kind*—that has ever lived on land.

Second, it had a body that was perfect for catching, killing, and eating lots of meat. Its head was so big that a human could fit inside. Lining its jaws were more than 50 thick teeth with razor-sharp edges. It stood proudly on two legs, its long tail balancing out its massive head. Its feet were big and broad, with claws on each toe. But its arms were tiny: although *T. rex* was the size of a bus, its arms were only the size of our own arms.

Third, *T. rex* ruled alone. It was by far the largest meat-eater of its time, and it didn't have to worry about sharing the top of the food chain with any other dinosaurs.

120

The king's diet

What did *T. rex* eat? Meat, of course. If your teeth look like knives and your fingers and toes have pointed claws, you're not eating cabbages. There is also direct fossil evidence for the type of meat that *T. rex* enjoyed. Skeletons of plant-eating dinosaurs like *Triceratops* and *Edmontosaurus* are often found with bite marks that perfectly match the size and spacing of *T. rex* teeth. So the king must have eaten these dinosaurs during the

Cretaceous. *T. rex* was so big that scientists think it may have needed to eat more than 200 pounds of meat every single day. That's more food than three or four lions, put together, eat on an average day!

When paleontologists began to find prey bones with *T. rex* bite marks, they noticed something unusual. While most theropods left simple scratches with their teeth, *T. rex* bites were big holes. The king, it seems, bit through the bones of its prey. This was later confirmed by the discovery of *T. rex* coprolites: its fossilized poop. These coprolites were full of bone chunks. Crushing the bones of your prey is not normal behavior: only a few animals alive today, like hyenas, can do it. So how was *T. rex* able to do it?

A *T. REX* EXPERIMENT

A clever experiment tells us how *T. rex* was able to bite through the bones of its prey. The experiment was designed by Greg Erickson, a paleontologist at Florida State University. Greg studies fossils together with modern animals. He also has a background in engineering. One day, while talking with some engineer friends, Greg came up with an idea. He would build a *T. rex* in the laboratory and measure how strong it could bite.

Greg didn't need to build the entire *T. rex* for his experiment to work. Instead, he made a perfect copy of a *T. rex* tooth out of bronze and aluminum. He then used a machine to push the metal tooth into the pelvis bone of a cow, which is very similar in shape to *Triceratops* bones that have been found with real *T. rex* bite marks. Greg pushed and pushed the tooth until it made a half-inch-deep hole that looked just like the real *T. rex* bite marks, and then he used a computer to measure the force that was required – 3,000 pounds per tooth!

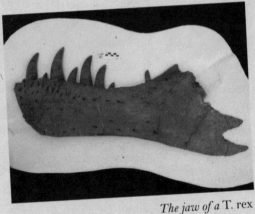

The jaw of a T. rex

Because its jaws were able to bite down with the force of 3,000 pounds! That's how much force a single *T. rex* tooth was able to produce – which is three times stronger than a lion's bite. It is equivalent to the weight of a pickup truck being dropped onto the prey of *T. rex*. And that is the force made by only one tooth! Remember, *T. rex* had more than fifty teeth in its mouth. When all these teeth worked together, powered by the huge muscles that opened and closed the jaws, they allowed *T. rex* to bite harder than any other animal that has ever lived on land. These strong bites were why *T. rex* was literally able to smash the bones of its prey.

This raises a problem. If *T. rex* had muscles and teeth that could break the bones of its prey, then it was also at risk of breaking its own skull bones when it bit into a *Triceratops*. This is basic physics: every reaction has an equal and opposite reaction. How did the king prevent such an injury?

DIGITAL *T. REX*

Emily Rayfield

123

Why was the skull of *T. rex* so strong? Sophisticated computer modeling provides the answer. This research was done by Emily Rayfield, a paleontologist at the University of

Bristol in England. Emily is one of the world's experts in using technology to study dinosaurs. Her lab is not full of fossils being removed from rock, but rather, it is a big, bright room with a row of computers.

Emily uses a technique called finite element analysis (FEA). It uses computer models to predict what will happen to something when a force is applied to it. This is very useful for engineers. For example, say you are an engineer tasked with building a bridge. You design a bridge that you think is perfect, but before you start building it with bricks and cement, you want to be sure that the bridge isn't going to collapse once heavy cars start driving over it. So to carefully check your plans, you can build a digital model of the bridge and use the computer to simulate the stresses of cars driving on it. You can then see how the bridge reacts. Does it handle the weight of the cars easily? Or does it start to crack under pressure? If it does start to crack, then the computer can identify the weak points, and you can go back to your plans and fix your mistake.

Emily does the same thing, but instead of bridges, she studies dinosaurs. She used a CAT scanner to make a digital model of a *T. rex* skull, and then put it into the FEA software. The software simulated what would happen when the *T. rex* bit with the force of a pickup truck on each tooth. Her study showed that the skull bones of *T. rex* fit together in a way that made them extra strong.

>>>

T. rex had a very strong skull that was perfect for dealing with the violent bites. The individual bones of the skull were tightly joined to one another, and some were even fused together entirely. Thick bars of bone surrounded the eye to protect it. The lower jaw was incredibly thick too. Added together, these features prevented the head of *T. rex* from tearing apart when it bit into its prey.

How did it move?

T. rex could bite very, very hard. Once it had a *Triceratops* or *Edmontosaurus* in its jaws, then it was game over. But how did it catch its prey? Not by running fast. *T. rex* was a special dinosaur in many ways, but one thing it could not do was run quickly. It probably moved at about 10 to 25 miles per hour. That's faster than we can run, but not as a quick as lions, cheetahs, or other top predators in today's world.

125

ANIMATING A *T. REX*

How do we know *T. rex* was a slow animal? Computers once again give us the answer. The world's expert on *T. rex* movement is John Hutchinson, an American paleontologist who now works at the Royal Veterinary College near London, England. In his lab, John studies modern animals, like elephants and giraffes, to better understand how they move. He then uses his knowledge of modern animals to build computer models of extinct species, like *T. rex*. The software he uses is similar to the programs used by animators who make movies.

To study *T. rex*, John used a laser to scan the bones of a skeleton, downloaded the scans to his computer, and then added muscles, skin, and other tissues based on his studies of modern animals. This produced an accurate digital model of *T. rex*. His software then checked what type of motion was possible, and calculated its speed. The result: 10 to 25 miles per hour. The software made clear why *T. rex* was so slow: it was simply too big to run any faster.

Because of this limitation, *T. rex* was not a chaser. It did not run down its prey over long distances. Instead, it probably was what we call an *ambush predator*. It would keep very still, perhaps by hiding in the forest. Maybe its body was even camouflaged green, so that it would match the color of the trees. It would watch its prey with its big, grapefruit-sized eyes. It would hear its prey with its sensitive ears. It would smell its prey with its big, powerful nose. Then, when the prey got close, the *T. rex* would jump out of the trees and pounce on it. Jaws would go into flesh, and the hunt was quickly over.

When it hunted, *T. rex* relied on its head to do most of the work. Many other meat-eating dinosaurs would use their arms to grab their prey and their claws to kill. But not *T. rex*. Its arms were far too small. What, then, did it use its arms for? This has been a mystery ever since the first *T. rex* skeletons were discovered.

As it turns out, those little arms – as silly as they may look – were not useless. Although the arms were short, they were stocky and muscular.

SOLVING THE MYSTERY OF THE TINY ARMS

Sara Burch

Paleontologist Sara Burch figured out why *T. rex*'s arms were so small, but still strong and muscular. Sara and I went to college together, and we both learned about dinosaurs by studying with Paul Sereno and working in his lab. After college, Sara did a PhD degree on dinosaur anatomy. Now she teaches medical students. Her knowledge of dinosaur bones and muscles helps her teach doctors about the human body!

Sara has a lab where she dissects birds, crocodiles, reptiles, and other modern animals. She uses scalpels to carefully cut open the animals and observe their insides, including muscles, hearts, lungs, and bones. By studying these animals, Sara can better understand dinosaurs. She can look at the modern animals and see where the muscles connect to bones. She can then look at dinosaur bones, recognize the scars and ridges where the muscles attached, and figure out how big and strong the dinosaur's muscles were and what movements they were capable of performing.

Sara studied the forearm muscles of *T. rex* and many other theropods. She realized that the arms of *T. rex* had big muscles for pulling the arms towards the body, meaning that it would have used its arms to hold on to prey while biting with its mouth.

T. rex actually had big, powerful shoulder and elbow muscles that pulled the arms toward the body. This means that *T. rex* would have been able to pull objects toward its chest, and hold them. *T. rex* probably used its short but strong arms to hold down struggling prey while the jaws crushed through bone. The arms did not capture or kill prey, but they helped the jaws do their work.

From baby to adult

By working together, the jaws and arms allowed *T. rex* to eat a lot of food. Because it ate so much, it could grow to such large sizes. And this raises another question: How quickly did *T. rex* grow from a baby into an adult?

Like all dinosaurs, *T. rex* reproduced by laying eggs. Baby *T. rexes* were tiny – probably no bigger than a pigeon – when they hatched from their eggs, which were most likely no larger than a football. Therefore, *T. rex* must have grown *a lot* to change from a little baby to an enormous adult.

Scientists used to think that *T. rex* grew like an iguana or a crocodile: that it kept growing throughout its life, gradually getting bigger and bigger and finally reaching its full adult size after about 100 years. Now we know that this is wrong. Dinosaurs like *T. rex* grew quickly, much more like birds than lizards or crocodiles.

The evidence is buried deep inside the bones of dinosaurs. Bones are made of living tissues, just like skin and muscle. As bone grows, new layers are added to the outside. If you cut open a dinosaur bone, you can see these different layers. They look like rings, and each ring marks one year of growth. So you can count the rings and tell how old the dinosaur was when it died. It's the same when you look at a tree trunk: you can count the rings and tell how old the tree is.

Greg Erickson, who earlier studied the bite force of

129

T. rex, cut open the bones of many dinosaurs, including *T. rex* and other tyrannosaurs. What Greg found shocked him. Not a single bone had more than thirty growth rings! That means tyrannosaurs hatched, grew up, reached adult size, and died within three decades. Their life span was less than half the average human life span. Thus, *T. rex* must have grown *very* quickly in order to get so big.

HOW FAST DID *T. REX* GROW?

How quickly did *T. rex* grow? To figure it out, Greg Erickson made a mathematical graph. For each *T. rex* fossil, he plotted its age (as told by the number of growth rings) against its size. This allowed Greg to determine how quickly *T. rex* grew each year. The answer is amazing: during its teenage years, from about ages ten to twenty, *T. rex* put on about 1,700 pounds (760 kilograms) per year. That's close to five pounds per day! No wonder *T. rex* had to eat so much. All that *Triceratops* and *Edmontosaurus* meat powered the teenage growth spurt that turned a kitty-sized hatchling into the King of the Dinosaurs.

Just like humans, the bodies of *T. rex* changed as they grew up. One of my best friends, Thomas Carr, has spent many years studying tyrannosaur growth. Thomas has carefully examined dozens of *T. rex* skeletons that have been found by paleontologists. These include fossils that cover the entire life of the dinosaur, from juvenile to adult. His research shows that *T. rex* was a long-legged, fast runner when it was young, but as an adult it got heavier and slower. Young *T. rexes* had long skulls with weak bones, small muscles, and thin teeth. But adults had deeper skulls with huge muscles and banana-sized teeth. It seems like juveniles could probably chase down prey like cheetahs do, but were not strong enough to crush through bone. Adults, on the other hand, couldn't run fast, but they had very powerful jaws.

Maybe the juveniles and the adults worked together. Perhaps they hunted in packs, with the juveniles chasing down the prey and then the adults jumping out at the last moment to kill the prey with a bone-shattering bite. This is a scary thought, but it is probably true. Paleontologists have found some tyrannosaur species in bonebeds, where many juveniles and adults are buried together as fossils. This is a sign that they were probably living together. And if they were living together, they were most likely hunting together.

T. rex in time

I could go on and on talking about *T. rex* because I think it was one of the most amazing animals that ever lived. But it did not live alone. It was part of a larger ecosystem of dinosaurs that thrived during the very end of the Cretaceous Period, around 67 to 66 million years ago. By this point in time, the small dinosaurs of the Triassic, the giant long-necked sauropods and Butcher *Allosaurus* of the Jurassic, and the carcharodontosaurs and tiny tyrannosaurs of the early Cretaceous were a distant memory. Time was marching on, the continents were moving farther apart, and *T. rex* ruled one corner of the globe while other dinosaurs thrived in other places. Let's meet some of these dinosaurs, the last survivors of the dinosaur empire.

9

Dinosaurs at the Top of Their Game: North America

Triceratops

TIMELINE: latest Cretaceous

ca. 72–66 million years ago

As terrifying as it was, *T. rex* was not a global supervillain. It lived in only one part of the world: western North America. No Asian, European, or South American dinosaurs lived in fear of *T. rex*. In fact, they never would have met a *T. rex*.

Remember that *T. rex* lived right at the end of the Age of Dinosaurs, between about 67 and 66 million years ago. Recall also that *T. rex* was one of many species of giant tyrannosaurs, which started to appear around 84 million years ago. This span of time – from 84 to 66 million years ago, during the latest part of the Cretaceous Period – was the glory days of the dinosaurs. There were more species than ever before, of many shapes and sizes, eating many different types of food, living all over the world.

And not only more species, *different* ones. The latest Cretaceous was a time of diversity. Even the biggest and most powerful dinosaurs, like *T. rex*, didn't live everywhere. Instead, each landmass had its own unique dinosaurs. As we learned a few chapters ago, the supercontinent of Pangea began breaking apart at the start of the Jurassic Period. Over the course of the Jurassic and Cretaceous periods, the new continents moved farther and farther apart from each other. By the end of the Cretaceous, the world map looked very similar to what it does today, with many smaller continents separated by oceans.

This was the world of *T. rex* and the other latest Cretaceous dinosaurs. North of the equator, there were two big landmasses: North America and Asia. South of the equator, the puzzle pieces of South America and Africa had just recently detached, and a narrow part of the Atlantic Ocean filled the gap between them. Antarctica sat at the bottom of the world, balanced on the South Pole. Off to its north was Australia. India, however, was very far from its present position. Although it is part of Asia today, in the latest Cretaceous, India was an island off the coast of Africa.

During this time, the Earth was hot. There were no ice caps or glaciers in the polar regions. Shallow seas extended far on to the land. One such sea drowned most of Europe, meaning only the tallest mountains stuck up as islands. Another sea cut North America into two: a western part and an eastern part. The western part is called Laramidia, and this was the hunting grounds of *T. rex*.

T. rex territory

Today, you can find many fossils of *T. rex* and the dinosaurs that it lived with. These fossils are found on the lands that used to make up Laramidia, which today are the western states of the USA and the western provinces of Canada. Some of the best fossils come from the badlands surrounding Hell Creek, in northeastern Montana. Hell Creek is a perfect name for this very hot area. It is a place of high humidity and mosquitoes, with rare breezes and little shade from the sun. There are rock bluffs that stretch to the horizon in all directions, which bake in the afternoon heat. But these bluffs contain treasure: lots and lots of dinosaurs!

Barnum Brown was one of the first explorers to visit Hell Creek on the search for dinosaurs. It was in Hell Creek rocks that he discovered the first skeleton of *T. rex* in 1902. After his prize discovery, Brown kept returning to collect more fossils.

Over time he understood why there are so many dinosaurs in the area. All the bones are found inside a thick sequence of colorful rocks, mostly mudstones and sandstones. Between about 67 and 66 million years ago, a tangle of rivers drained the Rocky Mountains to the west, and then moved across a vast plain and through forests, before emptying into that great seaway that cut North America in two. These were lush environments, perfect places for many dinosaurs to live. They were also perfect places to form rock: whenever the rivers flooded, they would bury the dinosaurs.

T. rex lived with many other dinosaurs on the ancient

plains of Hell Creek. One of these dinosaurs is also very famous: *Triceratops*.

Skull of a Triceratops

Three-horned face

Triceratops was the rival of *T. rex*. In many films, you'll see *T. rex* fighting *Triceratops*. *T. rex* is the fierce carnivore, hungry for blood. *Triceratops* is the gentle plant-eater, using its horns to protect itself from rex's bone-crunching bite. These battles would have actually happened because *T. rex* and *Triceratops* did live together. Their fossils are found together in the rocks of Hell Creek. Often, the *Triceratops* bones are covered in bite marks matching *T. rex* teeth, signs of their prehistoric fights.

HIGHWAY TO HELL CREEK

Hell Creek

I took my first trip to Hell Creek in 2005, when I was a college student. I was part of a crew from the Burpee Museum of Natural History, a small museum in Rockford, Illinois, which was close to where I grew up. Two childhood friends who now worked at the museum led the crew: Mike Henderson and Scott Williams. Scott was not a traditional scientist. He loved dinosaurs as a kid, but didn't have the opportunity to study paleontology in school. He ended up becoming a police officer, but he still found time to hunt for dinosaur bones during the summer. Eventually, he became so good at finding fossils that the museum gave him a job as a paleontologist.

I was in the back seat of Scott's car as he

drove the 1,000 miles from Rockford to the tiny town of Ekalaka, Montana. When we arrived, we moved into the wooden bunkhouses at Camp Needmore, deep in the cool pine forests that rose above the badlands. The first night I was kept awake by music coming from one of the cabins next door. The next morning, I met the man behind the music: Helmuth Redschlag. He was an architect, and for the summer holiday, he was joining the Burpee Museum team to look for dinosaurs.

'It makes me feel alive. The heat. The sun. Dinosaur bones!' Helmuth told me with a look of joy on his face.

A couple of days later, I was out prospecting with Scott, looking for any dinosaur bones sticking out of the rock. As our eyes were focused on the ground, Scott got an excited phone call from Helmuth.

'I found something!' Helmuth yelled through the phone. 'Bring the team and come quick!'

We raced over to find Helmuth a few miles down the road. We soon realized why he was so happy. Earlier that day, while he was prospecting, a dark brown bulge sticking out of the dull, tan-colored mudstone rocks caught his eye. He could tell that it was a bone, so he started to dig around it. By the time we arrived, he had already exposed a thighbone, several ribs and backbones, and part of the skull of a dinosaur!

We all crouched down to look at the bones.

Most of the skull bones were flat pieces in random shapes. They looked like shattered glass. A few others were sharp, pointy cones. Horns. Only one dinosaur in the Hell Creek ecosystem had skull bones like this: *Triceratops*, with three horns on its face and a broad, billboard-like frill extending from behind its eyes.

The more we looked, the more bones we saw. We kept digging, and eventually the site extended for nearly 700 square feet (64 square metres), and yielded more than 130 bones.

It quickly became very complex, so Scott asked me to make a map of all the bones. I laid out a metre-by-metre grid of string attached to chisels pounded into the rock. Using the grid for reference, I sketched the location of each bone in my field notebook. On the next page I identified each bone, gave it a number, and made notes on its size and position. After doing this for a while, we realized something strange.

'Wait a minute,' Scott said, with a puzzled look on his face. 'We have two of the same bone here. These are both nasal bones from the left side of the face. And here's another one! A third nasal bone!'

Then it dawned on us. Helmuth hadn't found a single *Triceratops*. He'd found three of them, buried together. It was a *Triceratops* graveyard!

This was the first time anybody had found more than one *Triceratops* in the same place. Until Helmuth saw that bone sticking out of the hill, we thought *Triceratops* always lived alone. And we were confident of that because *Triceratops* was so common. It was already known from hundreds of fossils found in Hell Creek rocks, for over a hundred years. Each fossil was a single individual, found on its own. But one discovery can change everything, and because of what Helmuth found, we now think that *Triceratops* was a pack species.

Triceratops is an ornithischian dinosaur: a member of the group of beaked, plant-eating species that first became common early in the Jurassic Period. The first ornithischians were small, fast-running animals with leaf-shaped teeth that they used to grind up plants. Then, sometime in the Jurassic, a new type of ornithischian evolved. These were the ceratopsians – the family that includes *Triceratops*.

The first ceratopsians were no bigger than dogs. They had sharp beaks at the front of their mouths, to snip leaves off branches, and rows of leaf-shaped teeth down their jaws, to chew up the leaves. They had a few small horns sticking out of their heads, which they probably used to attract mates or fight for territory. They walked mostly on their hind legs, and could run very fast. They needed to run, because the Jurassic world was full of predators like *Allosaurus*, which could swallow one of these small ceratopsians with a single gulp.

Over time, the ceratopsians got larger and larger. Their heads got bigger and wider. Their horns got longer and sharper. The biggest ceratopsians were animals like *Triceratops*, which weighed more than 10 tons, considerably bigger than a *T. rex*.

HOW *TRICERATOPS* WALKED

As the ceratopsians grew in size, their big heads became dangerous. They were so heavy that the ceratopsians risked falling over face-first. So they completely changed the way they stood and walked. Their bones and muscles were entirely reshaped.

Susannah Maidment, a British paleontologist, studied this transformation. She observed modern animals to predict what types of muscles ceratopsians would have had, and then added these muscles to computer models of ceratopsians. Susannah found that as ceratopsians got heavier over time, they began walking on all fours, to support their growing weight. They placed their feet slightly to the sides of their body, like you might do if you are walking on soft mud and need to keep your balance. Their extreme weight and four-legged stance meant that ceratopsians like *Triceratops* could not run very fast. But, most important, they could probably run a little bit faster than *T. rex*, so they were often one step ahead of their rival.

> > >

As ceratopsians got bigger and switched to walking on all fours, they also changed in other ways. Most notably, they started to develop a greater variety of horns and frills on their heads. *Triceratops* means 'three-horned face', in reference to the long horn over each eye and the single, smaller horn on top of its nose. This horn arrangement was unique to *Triceratops*. Other big ceratopsians had different types of horns. Some had a huge horn on their nose, others had large horns sticking sideways from the face, and some had dozens of little horns and spikes surrounding their frills. The bigger and stronger horns would have been good protection from the bite of a *T. rex* or other predators.

Many of these horns, however, were too small or thin to offer much security. Instead, these horns were probably used only for display. Ceratopsians used their horns like humans use hairstyles and clothes: to make themselves look attractive to mates, scary to rivals, and recognizable to other members of their species. Amazingly, we know how the horns of *Triceratops* grew. They were very small when a baby hatched from an egg, but then became big and showy once the *Triceratops* became old enough to start mating.

Big ceratopsians also developed a sophisticated way to eat lots of plants, using strange teeth. *Triceratops* had rows of many hundreds of teeth packed closely together,

144

forming what looked and functioned like a knife blade. There were four blades in total: one on each side of the upper jaw and one on each side of the lower jaw. When the jaws snapped shut, the blades from the top and bottom would slice past each other, like a giant pair of scissors. Any plants in the mouth would have been sliced and diced into tiny pieces.

HOW *TRICERATOPS* ATE

Ali Nabavizadeh

145

Paleontologist Ali Nabavizadeh is an expert on how *Triceratops* and its close relatives fed. While Ali was a student, he was able to dissect many large animals in his lab, including a rhinoceros and an elephant. These huge modern animals helped him understand how big ancient animals like *Triceratops* functioned. Ali found that *Triceratops* and its ceratopsian cousins developed enormous jaw-closing muscles, which both created a more powerful bite and helped cover the side of the mouth, like our cheeks.

Working together, the teeth and strong jaws would have allowed *Triceratops* to grab and break a large amount of leaves and stems, and keep them in the mouth, where they could be chewed into smaller pieces and then swallowed. *Triceratops* was a plant-eating machine. It was surely as good at eating plants as *T. rex* was at devouring meat.

There is something else remarkable about *Triceratops*: it lived in groups. We know this because of the discovery of a *Triceratops* graveyard by architect-turned-fossil-hunter Helmuth Redschlag (see p.139), during a field trip that I was part of. Some close cousins of *Triceratops* have been found in even bigger graveyards. One of these species, *Centrosaurus*, was found in a bonebed that was the size of nearly three hundred football fields and contains more than a thousand skeletons!

Therefore, it seems like these big, slow, horned, plant-munching ceratopsians were social species that lived together in herds. It brings to mind a beautiful image. These dinosaurs probably moved across western North America in vast herds of many thousands of individuals, rumbling the ground and kicking up clouds of dust as they plowed across the landscape. It probably would have looked similar to the herds of bison that would live on the same plains many millions of years later.

These *Triceratops* herds would have dominated the Hell Creek environment. If you were alive back then, you probably would have heard the sound of the herds before you saw them. While the herds were moving across the land, there would have been many hungry *T. rexes* hiding in the forests, in their own little hunting groups, waiting for the chance to strike.

The other dinosaurs of Hell Creek

But it wasn't only *Triceratops* and *T. rex* in Hell Creek. There were dozens of other kinds of dinosaurs too. We found many bones of these animals after Helmuth's discovery of the *Triceratops* graveyard. We discovered many teeth from smaller meat-eaters, including dromaeosaurid 'raptors' of the *Velociraptor* family.

147

The skull of a Velociraptor

We found the foot bones of human-sized theropods called oviraptorosaurs, which used beaks to eat a variety of food, from nuts and shellfish to plants and small mammals. There were also larger, cow-sized theropods with beaks called ornithomimosaurs. These dinosaurs had feathers – a story we'll get to later in the book.

Other fossils were from three distinct types of plant-eaters. The first was a fairly boring ornithischian called *Thescelosaurus*, about the size of a horse. The second was a slightly larger and much more interesting creature called *Pachycephalosaurus*, a dome-headed dinosaur with a skull the size of a bowling ball, which it used to headbutt its rivals in fights over mates and territory. The third was a big creature called *Edmontosaurus*, 7 tons in weight and about 40 feet (12 to 13 metres) long, with a sharp beak at the end of its long snout. It is a hadrosaur: a so-called duck-billed dinosaur.

All these dinosaurs were living together between about 67 and 66 million years ago, on that slice of western North America called Laramidia. Living with them were many crocodiles, lizards, frogs, flying reptiles called pterosaurs, and even mammals. But meanwhile, in other parts of the world, there were very different dinosaurs.

148

10

Dinosaurs at the Top of Their Game: Asia

Saurolophus

TIMELINE: latest Cretaceous

ca. 72–66 million years ago

At the same time that *T. rex* and *Triceratops* were fighting on the plains of ancient Hell Creek in the latest part of the Cretaceous Period, other dinosaurs were thriving in Asia.

Many of these Asian dinosaurs are similar, but not identical, to the North American species. For instance, there were large Asian meat-eaters like *Tarbosaurus* and *Alioramus*, which are both tyrannosaurs, and close cousins of *T. rex*.

As it turns out, many Asian dinosaurs at this time had close relatives in North America. It makes sense when you think about what the world looked like back then. Asia and North America were both in the northern hemisphere, as they are today. But in the latest Cretaceous, there were land bridges that connected both continents. This meant dinosaurs could move very easily between them.

The First expeditions

For many centuries, people have observed and collected dinosaur fossils across Asia. Specifically, many scientists have hunted for dinosaurs in the Gobi Desert, which covers parts of Mongolia and China today. During the

Late Cretaceous, this land was also a desert. There were sand dunes, with small pockets of trees, rivers, and lakes in between. Then at the very end of the Cretaceous, the deserts got wetter. Big rivers flowed through dense forests. Various dinosaurs lived in these different environments, and today their skeletons are found in the rocks that formed from the sand dunes and the rivers.

152

THE FIRST ASIAN DINOSAUR HUNTERS

Adrienne Mayor

Historian Adrienne Mayor spent many years reading stories told by ancient people. Well over 2,000 years ago, she discovered, travellers to central Asia wrote about mythical creatures called griffins, which looked like a combination of a lion and an eagle. Mayor thinks that the griffin is not entirely made up, but was based on fossil skeletons of the ceratopsian *Protoceratops* and other dinosaurs that these travellers came across. They noticed the bleached white skeletons of these dinosaurs poking out of red rocks, and then came up with a story to explain what they saw.

Over the last century, scientists have spent a lot of time digging up dinosaurs in the Gobi Desert. The first expeditions were launched in the 1920s. They were led by an American explorer and scientist named Roy Chapman Andrews, who worked at the American Museum of Natural History in New York.

FUN FACT

Roy Chapman Andrews

Some people think that Roy Chapman Andrews was the inspiration for the movie character Indiana Jones. Although this has never been confirmed, it's very possible. Andrews was a well-educated man who loved nature. He wore a wide-brimmed hat and loved traveling to remote corners of the world to look for treasure.

From 1922 until 1930, Andrews organized a series of expeditions to the Gobi Desert. These were not easy trips. The Gobi was still viewed as a wilderness, and very few Americans or westerners had ever journeyed there. Of course, many Mongolians called the desert home. Andrews met some of them, but mostly stuck with his own team of Americans, who travelled through the desert in a caravan of camels and automobiles – which at that time were new inventions. He was possibly the first paleontologist to use cars to hunt for fossils!

Andrews' team made many amazing discoveries. They found the first dinosaur nests, which proved that dinosaurs reproduced by laying eggs. They were the first scientists to discover skeletons of *Velociraptor*, the sharp-clawed meat-eater, and *Protoceratops*, a smaller cousin of *Triceratops*. They came across a totally new type of dinosaur, which they called *Oviraptor*. It was a theropod, a member of the diverse group of mostly meat-eating dinosaurs, including *T. rex* and *Velociraptor.* But *Oviraptor* didn't have any teeth! Instead, it had a beak, like a bird. It also had a strange crest of bone on its head, which it probably used for display. Andrews and his crew also found fossil mammals – some of our ancient ancestors.

New scientists explore the Gobi

Andrews wanted to keep working in the Gobi Desert, but after 1930 he was not allowed. The political situation in the region had changed, and China and the Soviet Union (the large country that once included Russia) now controlled most of the desert, and they did not want Americans there.

However, other scientists did continue working in the Gobi Desert. First, in the 1940s, teams of Russian researchers were given permission to travel even farther into the desert than Andrews. They found a wealth of fossils, including many skeletons of a new dinosaur they called *Tarbosaurus.* It looked nearly identical to *T. rex,* except for a few small differences in the skull. Basically, it is the Asian version of *T. rex.* It is *T. rex*'s closest cousin, and was the top predator that dominated Asian ecosystems at the end of the Cretaceous.

Then, in the early 1960s, a team of Polish scientists

began working with Mongolian scientists. A young paleontologist named Zofia Kielan-Jaworowska was asked to lead the team. This was a significant moment in the history of dinosaur research: Zofia was one of the first women to organize a major international expedition. She and her crew – which included several other young female scientists – had little experience working so far away from Poland, and many of them had never even been to a desert. But they prepared carefully, and worked closely with several young Mongolian-born scientists, like Demberlyn Dashzeveg and Rinchen Barsbold. Many people probably thought they would fail. But instead, they achieved enormous success.

156

Zofia's team went to the Gobi Desert nearly every year, from 1963 until 1971. They collected more than 20 tons of fossils, which they shipped back to Poland. Their prized discovery was the 'Fighting Dinosaurs' specimen: a *Velociraptor* fighting a *Protoceratops*, with the predator's sickle-shaped foot claw jammed into the neck of the plant-eater, which was trying to fight back when both of them were buried by a sudden storm. They also found many other dinosaurs: tyrannosaurs like *Tarbosaurus*, armour-covered ornithischians called ankylosaurs, giant long-necked sauropods, and duck-billed hadrosaurs.

MEETING A HERO

Zofia Kielan-Jaworowska

I was honored to meet Zofia Kielan-Jaworowska a few years before she died in 2015. When I was working in Poland with my friend Grzegorz Niedźwiedzki, who you may remember from the first chapter of this book, we visited Zofia at her home. She told me many stories of her adventures in the Gobi Desert. I listened quietly, in awe of her kind nature, her lifetime of discoveries, and the fact that she was very humble and gave a lot of credit to her many team members.

It was fitting that I met Zofia at this time, because I was right in the middle of working on my PhD studies with Mark Norell. It was Mark who eventually followed in Zofia's footsteps.

> > >

Beginning in the early 1990s, politics changed again, and Mongolia began to open up to the world. No longer did the Chinese and Soviets control all access to the country. Mark Norell, Mike Novacek, and colleagues from the American Museum of Natural History were invited to come to Mongolia and work with local scientists, some of whom had worked with Zofia a few decades earlier. They haven't stopped since. For over twenty-five years, they have gone to the Gobi Desert each summer. Their discoveries have been legendary too. They found an oviraptor sitting on its nest, protecting its eggs, just like birds do today. They found skulls and skeletons of *Velociraptor*, baby dinosaurs still inside their eggs, and countless new species of dinosaur, like the *Alioramus altai* skeleton that Mark asked me to study.

158

STUDYING ASIAN DINOSAURS

When I was twenty-four years old, I moved to New York City to study for my PhD degree at the American Museum of Natural History. On my first day, I went to lunch with Mark Norell, my adviser. Mark was one of the world's most respected dinosaur experts, and I was excited that I would get to learn from him for the next four and a half years.

Mark Norell

He told me about his adventures digging up fossils in the Gobi Desert of Mongolia, one of the world's harshest and driest places.

'I found an amazing dinosaur there,' he said as he told me about a new skeleton that he'd collected with his team. 'How would you like to study it?'

When we went back to the museum that afternoon, Mark took me to the lab, where several white boxes were laid out across a few tables. Each box had a carefully wrapped dinosaur bone inside. The bones were the color of rust and very fragile. They were somewhere between 72 and 66 million years old.

Mark carefully picked one up.

'Look at these teeth,' he said, pointing to a row of knife-sharp blades lining a jawbone. 'It's definitely a tyrannosaur, but I don't know what kind. I want you to tell me.'

I never imagined my first day of work would be so much fun!

Over the next few months I observed, measured, and photographed all the bones. I compared them to the bones of other dinosaurs. I confirmed that they did belong to a tyrannosaur, because they had characteristic features of tyrannosaurs like the fused nasal bones above the snout. But the new skeleton was different from the skeletons of T. rex and other tyrannosaurs. For example, it had a small horn sticking sideways from its cheek, which no other tyrannosaur had. It was also smaller than T. rex, and had a long snout.

I reported back to Mark with my findings, and he agreed. He suggested that we name it a new species, which we called *Alioramus altai*.

Duck-billed hadrosaurs

Mark Norell's teams have also found many skeletons of hadrosaurs: the duck-billed dinosaurs. These were important plant-eaters in both Asia and North America during the very end of the Cretaceous Period. We know that big tyrannosaurs like *T. rex* and *Tarbosaurus* liked to eat them because we often see tyrannosaur bite marks on hadrosaur bones. But the hadrosaurs were much more than simply prey. They were some of the most sophisticated dinosaurs to ever evolve.

Like *Triceratops* and the ceratopsians, the hadrosaurs are ornithischians: members of the big group of beaked, plant-eating dinosaurs. They also lived in vast herds, and their skeletons are often found together in bonebeds. They could stand on either all four legs, or only their hind legs. If they wanted to run, they might rear up on their hind legs, but if they wanted to move more slowly, they would get down on all fours. They could move quite fast, much faster than the heavy horned dinosaurs like *Triceratops*, and faster than *T. rex* and big tyrannosaurs too.

Most remarkably, many species had elegant crests made of bone sticking upward and backward from their skulls. Some were shaped like a helmet; others like an ax or a long pipe. The crests were probably used mostly for display, just like the horns of *Triceratops* and other ceratopsians. But there was one big difference: the crests of many hadrosaurs were hollow inside. The empty space was connected to the nose, which means that the hadrosaurs could have blown air through their crests. Why would they do this? Probably so they could make loud noises – like the sound a tuba makes – to communicate with each other over long distances.

161

Hadrosaurs are called duck-billed dinosaurs because they had broad, toothless bills at the front of their snout, like a duck.

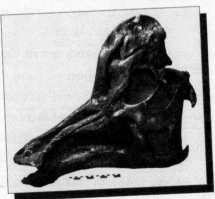

A hadrosaur skull.

They would have used these beaks to grab twigs and leaves. Then their large tongues would have passed this food to the back of the jaws, where it was chewed up by the teeth. Just like ceratopsians, hadrosaurs had hundreds of small teeth packed together into blades, which functioned like scissors. They may have even been able to move their jaws from side to side instead of only up and down, although paleontologists still debate about this. What is certain, however, is that hadrosaurs were very, very good at grabbing, chewing, and swallowing a lot of plants, very quickly. They were some of the most sophisticated plant-eaters that have ever evolved in the history of Earth.

162

Flowering plants

The hadrosaurs, and probably also the ceratopsians, had these incredible jaws for a reason. They were both eating a new type of plant that had evolved earlier in the Cretaceous: the angiosperms, more commonly known as the flowering plants.

Flowering plants are very common today. Much of our food (like tomatoes, corn, and lettuce) comes from flowering plants as well as many of the beautiful trees, shrubs, and bushes that decorate our gardens. However, the first dinosaurs in the Triassic, and even the huge sauropods of the Jurassic, would have never seen these plants. Flowering plants show up as fossils in rocks that date from the early part of the Cretaceous Period. Afterward, they began to grow larger and spread around the world. By the end of the Cretaceous, flowering plants were the preferred food for many types of dinosaurs.

It is quite the scene to think about. The Gobi Desert, 66 million years ago. It was green and full of life, not hot and covered in sand. Hadrosaurs were chewing on flowers, living in the dense forests to hide from the tyrannosaurs that preyed on them. Oviraptors guarded their nests and took care of their babies, while raptors hid in the bushes, waiting to attack. A giant sauropod or two lumbered by, shaking the ground as it slowly moved along the river.

This was a time when dinosaurs still ruled the world.

11

Dinosaurs at the Top of Their Game: The South

Carnotaurus

TIMELINE: latest Cretaceous

ca. 72–66 million years ago

During the latest Cretaceous, dinosaurs lived not only in North America and Asia. They lived across the southern continents too. New fossil discoveries in countries like Brazil tell scientists what these dinosaurs looked like and how they evolved.

Almost smack in the middle of Brazil is a stretch of flat land called Goiás. It is farming country, with fields of corn and soybeans extending in every direction, as far as the horizon. But it also holds many secrets.

Underneath the farms is a hidden landscape, one that was on the surface during the latest part of the Cretaceous Period, between about 86 and 66 million years ago. It is a landscape of windy deserts on the edges of great river valleys. This was a paradise for dinosaurs. Their bones can today be found in the 1,000-foot-thick basement of rocks, formed in the deserts and rivers, which now lie underground.

At the same time these dinosaurs were living in Brazil, *T. rex* was fighting *Triceratops* in North America, and *Tarbosaurus* was hunting duck-billed dinosaurs in Asia. But you won't find these species in Brazil. By the end of the Cretaceous, the southern continents were so far separated from the northern continents that very few dinosaurs could move between them.

DIGGING DINOSAURS IN BRAZIL

Roberto Candeiro

I first visited Brazil in 2016, invited by Roberto Candeiro, a professor in Goiás. Roberto asked me to join a field trip with him and several of his students. Our mission was to find bones of these latest Cretaceous dinosaurs, so we could better understand what species were living in Brazil, and what their world was like.

For many hours, we drove across the lonely highways of Goiás, past farmers on tractors and barns where grain was being stored. Finally, we pulled up to a gate and began driving down a narrow road into a big hole in the ground. We were going into a quarry, where locals were mining Cretaceous-aged rock to sprinkle on their fields as fertilizer, to help the crops grow better.

We stopped and Roberto began handing out small plastic shields, which looked like the shin

168

guards football players use to protect their legs.

'This is very important!' Roberto said. 'Put these on now. They will protect you from the snakes.'

I was frightened, but none of Roberto's students were. They were all from Brazil, and used to doing fieldwork in these conditions.

Over the next few days I got to know the team, which reflected the diversity of their country. I became particularly friendly with Andre, a funny man who was back in school after working on the farms, and Camila, a young woman who had moved from the big city to study fossils with Roberto. They were the new generation of Brazilian paleontologists, the people who will be making dinosaur discoveries for many decades to come.

We looked for bones, but sadly, we didn't find very much. All I found on the trip was one single bone, which was so broken that I couldn't identify it. That's how it goes sometimes: you go to the right places, with the right kinds of rocks that should have dinosaur bones, but you still don't find anything special.

After the field trip, we went to Roberto's lab at the university in Goiás. Now, finally, I saw dinosaur bones. Roberto's lab was full of them. Although our trip had not been successful, Roberto and his students have gone on many other expeditions over the past few years, and they have collected many important fossils.

> > >

Nobody has ever found a bone, tooth, or footprint of a latest Cretaceous tyrannosaur from South America, Africa, Australia, Antarctica, India, or any of the other modern places that make up the former southern land-mass of Gondwana.

Instead, the southern lands had their own unique dinosaurs – including some giant carnivorous dinosaurs – but these were different species, members of totally different groups. One of these groups we've already met: the carcharodontosaurs, that clan of mighty meat-eaters that terrorized much of the Earth earlier in the Cretaceous. Carcharodontosaurs once lived in North America and Asia, but they went extinct and were replaced by tyrannosaurs. Not so in the south. In Brazil and elsewhere south of the equator, the carcharodontosaurs hung on and remained at the top of the food chain for much, much longer.

And they were joined by another type of predator, called abelisaurids. These dinosaurs have been found in Brazil and Argentina, and also in other places that used to be south of the equator in the latest Cretaceous, like Madagascar, Africa, and India. Some of the most famous abelisaurids are species like *Carnotaurus*, *Majungasaurus*, and *Skorpiovenator*.

These were fierce animals, a little bit smaller than

The skull of an abelisaurid

tyrannosaurs and carcharodontosaurs, but still at or near the top of the food chain.

Abelisaurids had short and deep skulls, sometimes with stubby horns jutting out from near the eyes. The bones of the face and snout had a rough texture, which was probably covered by a film of keratin, the same material that makes up our fingernails. They walked on two muscular legs like *T. rex*, but had even more pitiful forearms. The abelisaurid *Carnotaurus* was 30 feet (9 metres) long and weighed 1.6 tons, but had arms barely bigger than a kitchen spatula! It seems that these arms just flopped around in a useless way. Clearly the abelisaurids didn't need their arms. They relied on their jaws and their teeth for all the dirty work.

What did the southern predators eat?

That dirty work, for both abelisaurids and carcharo-dontosaurids, was catching and chomping the other dinosaurs they lived with, particularly the plant-eaters. Some of them were similar to northern species – for example, some duck-billed dinosaurs have been found in Argentina. But for the most part, it was a different bunch of herbivores down south. There were no vast herds of ceratopsians like *Triceratops*, and no dome-headed pachycephalosaurs headbutting each other. There were, however, sauropods. Hordes of them. In Brazil and the other southern lands, sauropods remained the primary large-bodied plant-eaters, right up to the end of the Cretaceous.

It was one particular type of sauropod that spread across the south: the titanosaurs. Some were truly epic in proportions. *Austroposeidon*, which was discovered south of Goiás in São Paulo State, is the largest dinosaur ever found in Brazil. Each backbone is the size of a bathtub! The entire creature was probably about 80 feet (25 metres) long from snout to tail, and weighed somewhere around 20 to 30 tons, or maybe much more.

Other titanosaurs, however, were considerably smaller. The so-called aeolosaurins were modest creatures, at least as sauropods go. Some of the better-known species, like *Rinconsaurus*, were merely 4 tons in weight and 36 feet (11 metres) long. Another group of small sauropods, called saltasaurids, protected themselves from hungry abelisaurids and carcharodontosaurs with armour plates in their skin.

We also know that there were some smaller theropods that lived in Brazil at this time. Some of these were meat-eaters, and some were omnivores that ate all kinds of food. Compared to North America and Asia, however, these small theropods were rare.

There seems to be a good explanation. In Brazil, Roberto and his colleagues find many skeletons of small meat-eaters and omnivores, but they are not theropods. Instead, they are crocodiles. Some of these crocs lived in the water, like today's species. Others had long legs and could run fast, like a dog. Some had sharp teeth to eat meat, others broader teeth to grind plants. One croc even had a body covered in armour, and could roll itself up in a ball to protect itself from predators. So in Brazil and across the south, it seems like the crocs were filling similar roles as theropod dinosaurs in the north.

173

Southern dreams

Let yourself imagine the scene, about 66 million years ago, south of the equator. There were huge carcharodontosaurs and abelisaurids instead of tyrannosaurs, sauropods instead of *Triceratops*, and swarms of crocs instead of raptors. It was a different world, but still a world in which dinosaurs were thriving. It was their world – this was their normal, and to these southern dinosaurs, a *T. rex* would have seemed strange.

174

12

Dinosaurs at the Top of Their Game: Europe

Balaur

TIMELINE: latest Cretaceous

ca. 72–66 million years ago

North America, Asia, and South America were all big continents during the latest Cretaceous. But remember that sea levels were higher back then, and parts of the world that are dry land today were mostly flooded. The main example is Europe.

Today Europe is a big continent that extends towards Asia. During the end of the Cretaceous, though, Europe was covered by water. Some specks of land did stick out from above the waves, as islands. Cretaceous Europe was similar to the Caribbean today: a lot of small islands, in the middle of a warm, tropical sea. Living on these islands were some very, very strange dinosaurs.

The first person to study these dinosaurs was Franz Nopcsa von Felső-Szilvás, a member of a European royal family (see p.178). Nopcsa collected many fossils on the lands that his family owned in what is now Romania, and he compared them to dinosaurs that lived at the same time in North America. He realized something very puzzling.

THE DINOSAUR BARON

Franz Nopcsa

Franz Nopcsa von Felső-Szilvás was one of the most extraordinary paleontologists who has ever lived. Nopcsa was a baron – a member of a royal family – in the Austro-Hungarian empire that used to span much of Europe.

Nopcsa was born in 1877 in the gentle hills of Transylvania, which is now part of Romania, but was then on the edge of the Austro-Hungarian empire. He spoke many languages and loved to travel deep into the mountains. Nopcsa's travels were not all innocent, and he had many secrets. He worked as a spy for his empire around the time of World War I; he and his boyfriend smuggled guns and tried to form an army to defeat the Turks, and he even tried to make himself king of Albania. All those schemes failed, so Nopcsa turned to other things to occupy his time.

178

He became obsessed with dinosaurs.

In fact, Nopcsa became interested in dinosaurs before he started spying and fighting. When he was eighteen years old, his sister picked up a fossil skull on the family estate. Nopcsa brought it with him when he started studying at the university later that year, and his professor was intrigued. He told Nopcsa to go out and collect more bones, which the young baron did. He explored the fields, hills, and riverbeds of his royal land. Four years later, while still a student, he made a big announcement to a room full of famous professors. He told them he had found a whole ecosystem of strange dinosaurs – many of which were smaller than their cousins that lived in other places during the latest Cretaceous.

Nopcsa's dwarf dinosaurs

Nopcsa could tell that his dinosaurs belonged to groups that were common in other parts of the world. For example, a new species that he named *Telmatosaurus* was a duck-billed dinosaur. A long-necked plant-eater called *Magyarosaurus* was a sauropod. He also found the bones of armoured dinosaurs.

But all these dinosaurs were unusual: they were smaller than their mainland relatives. In some cases, the difference was astounding. At the same time its cousins were shaking the Earth with their 30-ton bodies in Brazil, *Magyarosaurus* was barely the size of a cow!

At first Nopcsa thought the bones belonged to babies, but when he put them under a microscope, he realized they had the characteristic bones of adults. There was only one possible explanation: these Transylvanian dinosaurs were miniatures.

This raised an obvious question: Why were they so tiny? Nopcsa had an idea. Along with his expertise in studying fossil bones, Nopcsa was also a very good geologist. He mapped the rocks that held the dinosaur fossils and could tell that they formed in rivers. But underneath these rocks were other layers that came from the ocean – clays and shales bursting with microscopic plankton fossils.

Nopcsa put the clues together and realized that his royal estate used to be part of an island, which emerged from the water sometime during the latest Cretaceous. The mini dinosaurs were living on a small bit of land, probably around 30,000 square miles (80,000 square kilometers) in area, about the size of modern-day Hispaniola (the island that includes the Dominican Republic and Haiti).

Nopcsa then had a brilliant idea. Maybe the dinosaurs were small *because* of their island habitat.

Strange, small animals live on many islands in the modern world. This is because islands are laboratories of evolution, where some of the normal rules of larger continents don't apply. There is less space on islands, meaning there are fewer resources like food and water. This can cause animals living on the island to get smaller over time. Also, islands are cut off from the mainland. Thus, the plants and animals on islands can evolve on their own, in isolation, becoming more different from their continent-living cousins over time. It was for these reasons, Nopcsa thought, that his island-living dinosaurs were so small.

Today, we realize that Nopcsa was correct.

Where are the meat-eaters?

There was one thing that Nopcsa didn't know about. Almost every bone he found – whether sauropod, duckbill, or armoured ankylosaur – came from a plant-eater. What predators ate his dwarfed dinosaurs?

181

Solving this mystery took a century, and another remarkable scientist from Transylvania, Mátyás Vremir (see below).

While collecting fossils with his sons, Mátyás found the skeleton of a little dinosaur, only about the size of a poodle. What type of dinosaur was it?

MÁTYÁS THE ADVENTURER

Mátyás Vremir lived in Romania. He spoke many languages and travelled around the world. Mátyás was a geologist who ran his own company that advised the government on building projects. But he also liked exploring caves and fossil collecting,

Mátyás Vremir

and Mátyás was one of the best fossil finders that I knew.

In the autumn of 2009, Mátyás and his two young sons were walking along a river when he saw some white lumps poking out from the red rocks of the riverbank. They were bones! He took out his tools and scratched into the soft rock, and more bones kept appearing. Before long he had exposed the limbs and chest area of a small dinosaur.

His excitement turned to fear. The local power station was beginning to empty a lot of water into the river, and soon the currents would cover up the bones. So Mátyás worked quickly but carefully, and cut the skeleton out of its

69-million-year-old tomb. He brought it back to Cluj-Napoca, the city he lives in, and made sure it was kept safe in the local museum.

Then it was time to figure out what the skeleton was. Mátyás was pretty sure it was a dinosaur, but nothing like it had been found in Transylvania before. He thought some advice would be useful, so he emailed Mark Norell in New York. Mark, you might recall, is the famous paleontologist who discovered many dinosaurs in the Gobi Desert in Asia.

When Mark received the email from Mátyás, he called me into his office. Our jaws both dropped as we looked at the photos on the screen. The skeleton was beautiful. Most of the bones were there – almost everything except for the head. We thought it belonged to a small theropod, but we needed to see the actual fossils to be sure.

A few months later, Mark and I went to Romania and met with Mátyás and another Romanian scientist, a young professor named Zoltan Csiki-Sava. Mátyás brought out the skeleton. For the next week we looked at the bones together. We photographed them, measured them, and compared them to other dinosaurs. We then identified the bones as belonging to a new species, which we called *Balaur bondoc*.

Many of its light, delicate bones resembled those of *Velociraptor*. It was about the same size as *Velociraptor* too, or maybe even a little smaller. That means it was a meat-eating theropod. Finally, here was the clue that Nopcsa never found!

But something didn't quite fit. Mátyás's dinosaur had four big toes on each foot, and the two inner ones had huge, sickle-shaped claws. Raptor dinosaurs were famous for these claws, which they used to slash and kill their prey. But all raptors had only a single claw on each foot. Plus, they had only three main toes, and not four.

There was only one good explanation. This new Romanian theropod was a raptor, but a peculiar one, with extra toes and claws compared to its mainland relatives.

This solved Nopcsa's mystery. While the plant-eating dinosaurs of the ancient Transylvanian island got small, the predators went weird. It wasn't just the double set of killer claws and the extra toe that set Mátyás's raptor apart. It was bulkier than *Velociraptor*, many of the bones of its arms and legs were fused together, and it had even had a small hand that was reduced to a mass of stubby finger and wrist bones. The Romanian raptor was a new species of meat-eating dinosaur, and a few months later I worked with Mátyás to give it a fitting scientific name: *Balaur bondoc*. The first word is an old Romanian term for dragon, and the second means 'stocky'.

Balaur bondoc was the top predator of the European islands during the latest Cretaceous. It was no mighty tyrant, but more of a silent killer.

Balaur would employ its claws to eat the cow-sized sauropods and mini duck-billed dinosaurs stuck in the middle of the rising ocean.

The foot of a Balaur

Best we can tell, it was the largest meat-eating dinosaur on the islands. The islands were simply too small for giant bone-crunching monsters like *T. rex*, so it was feisty little critters like *Balaur* that topped the food chain.

The dinosaurs of Europe were unique during the latest Cretaceous. So were the dinosaurs of South America and the southern continents, and North

America, and Asia. But although different species lived on these lands, one thing was constant. All the continents were all dominated by dinosaurs. Dinosaurs were ruling the world, everywhere.

13

Dinosaurs Take Flight

Archaeopteryx

TIMELINE: Late Jurassic–Today

ca. 150 million years ago–today

The dinosaurs we learned about in the previous chapters – *T. rex* and *Triceratops* from North America, the Asian duck-bills, the titanosaurs of Brazil, *Balaur bondoc* and the dwarfed dinosaurs of Europe – all lived millions of years ago. And they are extinct. You might think that all dinosaurs are extinct. But that's not the case!

There is actually a dinosaur outside my window. I'm watching it as I write this.

It is a real, living, breathing, moving dinosaur, a descendant of those little dinosauromorphs that emerged onto Pangea 250 million years ago. It is part of the same family tree as *Brontosaurus* and *Triceratops*, and a close cousin of *T. rex* and *Velociraptor*.

This dinosaur is about the size of a house cat, but with long arms tucked against its chest, and a much shorter pair of skinny legs, with scale-covered feet. Most of its body is white, but the edges of its arms are grey, and the tips of its hands are black. It is perched on my neighbor's rooftop, its head arching upward, standing out against the darkening clouds of eastern Scotland.

When the sun breaks through, I catch a sparkle reflecting from its eyes, which start to dart back and forth. No doubt this is a smart creature with strong senses. It's on to something. Maybe it can tell that I'm watching.

Then, without warning, it opens its mouth and emits a high-pitched screech. Maybe it is trying to communicate with some of its other dinosaur friends. Or maybe it is trying to threaten me, to make me look away.

The air becomes silent again, and the fluffy-coated critter turns its neck so that it's now staring directly at me. It definitely knows I'm here. Expecting another shriek, I'm surprised when it closes its mouth, its jaws coming together to form a sharp yellow beak. It doesn't have any teeth, but this beak looks like a nasty weapon that could do a lot of damage.

190

And then the creature makes its move. It pushes its webbed feet off the roof tiles, extends its feathered arms outward, and leaps into the breeze. I lose sight of it as it disappears over the trees, probably on its way to the North Sea.

The dinosaur I'm watching is a seagull. There are thousands of them living around Edinburgh, often diving for fish in the sea a couple of miles north. Occasionally I catch one of them dive down on an unsuspecting tourist, spearing a chip or two with its beak before launching back into the sky. When I observe this type of behavior – the intelligence, the agility, the nastiness – it's easy to see the inner *Velociraptor* in an otherwise forgettable seagull.

It is true. Seagulls, and all other birds, evolved from dinosaurs. That makes them dinosaurs. Put another way, birds can trace their heritage back to the common ancestor of dinosaurs, and therefore are 'dinosaurs' in the same way that *T. rex*, *Brontosaurus*, or *Triceratops* are. Birds are one of the many branches on the dinosaur family tree.

This is a very important concept, so I will repeat it. *Birds are dinosaurs.* Yes, it can be hard to believe it. I often get people who try to argue with me. Sure, these people say, birds might have evolved from dinosaurs, but they are so different from *T. rex*, *Brontosaurus*, and the other familiar dinosaurs that we shouldn't classify them in the same group. This might seem like a reasonable argument. But I always have a quick reply.

191

Think about bats. Bats are strange animals. They look different from foxes or elephants or mice. But they are mammals because they evolved from other mammals, and have all the characteristic mammal features like hair, and they make milk for their young. They are just an unusual type of mammal that evolved wings and developed the ability to fly.

You should think about birds in a similar way. Birds are just an unusual type of dinosaur that evolved wings and developed the ability to fly.

We're so used to saying that dinosaurs are extinct, but that's not really true. Indeed, the vast majority of dinosaurs died 66 million years ago, when that latest Cretaceous world of *T. rex* vs. *Triceratops* was plunged into chaos. We'll get to that story in the next chapter. But a few brave dinosaurs survived – birds. The descendants of those survivors live on today as more than 10,000 species. They live all over the planet. Sometimes we keep them as pets, and sometimes we eat them as food (think about that the next time you're eating chicken!). Dinosaurs, thus, are still an important part of our world.

Many people ask me two questions about the dinosaur–bird connection. First, how do we know that birds evolved from dinosaurs? And second, how exactly did evolution take a dinosaur and turn it into a small, feathered, winged bird that could fly? By answering these questions, paleontologists can show they are certain that birds are dinosaurs.

How do we know birds evolved from dinosaurs? The first evidence

The idea that birds evolved from dinosaurs is not new. It goes back to the 1860s, when Charles Darwin first described how evolution works through a process called natural selection. He explained it in his famous book, *The Origin of Species.*

DARWIN'S THEORY OF EVOLUTION

This is how evolution by natural selection works. All members of a species are slightly different from each other. For instance, if you look at a bunch of rabbits in nature, they will have slightly different fur colours, even if they all belong to the same species. Sometimes one of those varieties makes it easier for an individual to survive. For example, darker fur might help a rabbit camouflage itself better, so it can better avoid being eaten by predators. Because of that, the rabbits with darker fur have a better chance of living longer and having more babies than rabbits with lighter fur. If the darker fur can be passed on to offspring, then over time it will spread throughout the whole population, so that now the entire rabbit species is dark-haired. Dark hair has been *naturally selected*, and the rabbits have evolved.

This process can even produce new species. If a population is somehow divided and each group goes its own way, evolving its own naturally selected features until the two subsets are so different that they are unable to reproduce with each other, then they have developed into separate species. Over billions of years, this process can explain how all the world's species came to be.

> > >

When Darwin presented his theory, people were skeptical. Darwin and his supporters knew that people would need proof, so they went searching for so-called *link fossils*. These are fossils that capture the evolution of one type of animal into another. In other words, they are fossils with a mixture of the characteristic features of two different groups of animals: the ancestor and the new animal that is evolving.

Darwin didn't have to wait long. In 1861, quarry workers in Germany found something peculiar as they were mining a type of fine limestone that breaks into thin sheets. One of the miners split open a slab and found a 150-million-year-old skeleton of a puzzling creature inside. It had sharp claws and a long tail like a reptile, but feathers and wings like a bird. Other fossils of the same animal were soon found in other nearby limestone quarries, including a spectacular one that preserved nearly the entire skeleton. This one had a wishbone at the front of its chest, like a bird, but its jaws were lined with sharp teeth, like a reptile. Whatever this creature was, it seemed to be half reptile, half bird. It was a link fossil!

This Jurassic-aged hybrid was named *Archaeopteryx*. It caught the eye of one of Darwin's best friends, scientist Thomas Henry Huxley. Huxley agreed that *Archaeopteryx* was a link fossil, connecting reptiles and birds, but he went one step further. He noticed that it looked very similar to another skeleton discovered in the same limestones: a small flesh-eating dinosaur called *Compsognathus*. So he proposed his own radical new idea: birds descended from dinosaurs.

New evidence emerges

Debate continued for the next century. Some scientists followed Huxley, while others didn't accept the link between dinosaurs and birds. In the 1960s, paleontologists began to discover the bones of raptor dinosaurs: theropods like *Velociraptor* and *Deinonychus*, which in many ways looked like large birds. They had long arms that looked almost like wings, slender bodies that could clearly move very fast, and big brains. But still, some scientists did not accept the growing evidence. They needed more proof. That final proof came in 1996.

195

While out working his fields in the northeastern Chinese province of Liaoning, a farmer broke open a rock. Inside was a small dinosaur, clearly a fast-running, meat-eating theropod. Most of the bones of the skeleton were there, beautifully preserved. Surrounding the bones was a coat of fluff – feathers! Only one type of animal today has feathers: birds. This ended the debate once and for all: if some dinosaurs had feathers, then birds must have evolved from dinosaurs.

This fossil was named *Sinosauropteryx*. It was the

start of something special. Scientists sprinted to Liaoning, and within a few years, farmers from across the countryside had reported several other feather-covered dinosaur species, which were given names like *Caudipteryx*, *Protarchaeopteryx*, *Beipiaosaurus*, and *Microraptor*. Today, a little over two decades later, more than twenty such species are known. These are represented by thousands of individual fossils.

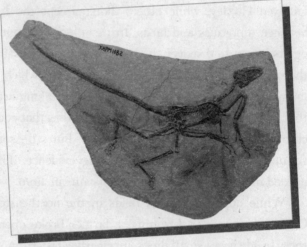

Fossil of a Microraptor

These dinosaurs had the bad luck to live in a dense forest near powerful volcanoes. Occasionally the volcanoes would erupt, and the ash would combine with water to flood the forests in a sticky ooze that buried everything in sight. That's why the details of the feathers are so perfect.

The feathered dinosaurs of Liaoning are the best evidence that birds evolved from dinosaurs. More than any other single clue, they answer the first question I posed above. They also tell the story of *how* birds evolved from dinosaurs. This answers my second question.

How did evolution take a dinosaur and turn it into a small, feathered, winged bird that could fly?

To begin to answer this, we need to know how birds fit in with other dinosaurs. The feathered dinosaurs of Liaoning confirm that birds are a type of theropod: they are part of that group of ferocious meat-eaters that includes *T. rex* and *Velociraptor,* along with many of the other predators that we've learned about in earlier chapters, like *Allosaurus,* carcharodontosaurs, and abelisaurids. We know this because today's birds share many features with theropods: not just feathers, but also wishbones that connect the two shoulder girdles and three-fingered hands that can fold against the body, along with hundreds of other aspects of the skeleton.

The closest theropod relatives of birds are raptors like *Velociraptor, Deinonychus,* and *Zhenyuanlong.* The raptors traded the strength and size of their *T. rex*-like ancestors for bigger brains, sharper senses, and lighter skeletons that allowed them to be more active and fast-moving.

Today's birds stand out among all modern animals.

197

They have feathers, wings, toothless beaks, wishbones, big heads that bob along on an S-shaped neck, hollow bones, toothpick legs, and the list goes on. These signature features define what we call the bird *body plan*: the unique things that make a bird a bird. This body plan is behind the many superskills that birds are so renowned for: their ability to fly, their very fast growth, their high intelligence and sharp senses. Somehow, birds must have evolved this entire body plan from their theropod ancestors.

The feathered dinosaurs of Liaoning tell us how. Many of the supposedly unique features of today's birds — the components of their body plan — first evolved in their dinosaur ancestors. Far from being unique to birds, these features developed much earlier, in theropods. These features did not evolve to specifically help birds fly, but for other reasons. They also did not all evolve at the same time, but one by one. To understand it, let's talk more about feathers.

Feathers and wings

Feathers didn't suddenly develop when the first birds came about and started to fly. Rather, feathers originally evolved in the distant dinosaur ancestors of birds. These earliest feathers, however, looked very different from the quill pens that make the wings of modern birds. The feathers of *Sinosauropteryx* and most other Liaoning dinosaurs were more like fluff, made up of thousands of simple, straight, hairlike strands. There was no way these dinosaurs could fly. Their feathers were too simple and they didn't even have wings. It would be like you or me trying to fly with our hair! Impossible. So the first feathers must have evolved for something else, probably to keep these small dinosaurs warm, or maybe as a way to camouflage their bodies.

For most dinosaurs, a coat of simple feathers was enough. But one group of theropods – the raptors – started to change. The hairlike strands became longer. They then started to branch, first into a few simple branches and then later into many extensions called *barbs* that project sideways from a central shaft. These quill-pen feathers were lined up and layered across each other on the arms, forming wings. Perhaps surprisingly, many raptor dinosaurs had wings. Even *Velociraptor* itself!

You might think that wings evolved specifically for flight. But we now know that dinosaurs evolved wings for other reasons first, and only later did they start to use them to fly. Two remarkable pieces of evidence tell us that this is the case.

The first wings start showing up in raptors and other theropod dinosaurs that were far too big to fly. The earliest dinosaurs to evolve wings were ornithomimosaurs, a type of theropod that ate bugs and plants with their sharp beaks.

A team in Canada, led by Darla Zelenitsky, came across the skeleton of an ornithomimosaur, its body surrounded by dark streaks that looked like fuzzy hair, and its arms lined with larger pen-like shapes. At first Darla and her team didn't know what the structures were, but then they found two more skeletons, each with the same features. When looked at closely, the scientists could see these structures were identical to the feathers of Liaoning dinosaurs like *Sinosauropteryx*.

The first feathered dinosaurs outside of China had been found!

These ornithomimosaurs were the size of a horse, and their wings were no bigger than a computer screen. They could not have used such tiny wings to keep their big bodies afloat in the air. The wings must have evolved for another reason.

But why? A second clue suggests an answer. In the late 2000s, a student named Jakob Vinther began to look at fossils under high-powered microscopes. He kept seeing many bubble-like structures, invisible to the naked eye because they are so small. These fossil bubbles were identical to structures called melanosomes, found in modern animals. These are the capsules that hold pigment, the stuff that gives animals their colours. Melanosomes of different sizes and shapes result in different colours. Sausage-shaped ones make a black colour, meatball-shaped ones a rusty red, and so on.

This unlocked an amazing possibility: by studying dinosaur melanosomes, you could tell what colour the dinosaurs were!

It turns out that the feathers and wings of the first, non-flying dinosaurs were a rainbow of different colours. Black, brown, grey, white, red. Some had camouflage patterns, others stripes and bands, and others even had shiny feathers. Colourful feathers and wings like these would have been perfect display structures. Like the tail of a peacock, they were not used for flight, but to attract mates and scare away rivals.

Birds take flight

All this evidence shows that feathers, and even wings, did not evolve for flying. Wings, it seems, developed first as advertising billboards sticking out of the arms of some dinosaurs. Over time, as the wings got bigger and the dinosaurs got smaller, something interesting happened. When the dinosaurs started to move these wings, they could hold themselves up in the air a little bit. These first attempts at flight were most likely very awkward. Different dinosaurs probably used their wings in different ways: some flapped their arms, others merely stuck out their arms and glided in the air currents. But the important thing was that dinosaurs were now flying. At this point, evolution could continue to do its work, and over time these dinosaurs were moulded into better and better fliers.

Birds had finally evolved! And now they had access to new places to live, feed, and make nests. These first birds began to spread around the world and evolve into many new species. All this was happening back in the Jurassic Period, probably between about 170 and 150 million years ago. This means that birds lived alongside their dinosaur ancestors for about 100 million years, before surviving the extinction that killed off *T. rex*, *Triceratops*, and all the other dinosaurs 66 million years ago.

What were these first birds like?

JINGMAI THE BIRD EXPERT

Jingmai O'Connor

Jingmai O'Connor is a young paleontologist. She was born in America, but now works in China, where she has studied thousands of birds found alongside the feathered dinosaurs of Liaoning. She is widely regarded as the world's leading expert on the oldest fossil birds. She has described over a dozen new species of ancient birds, and even found part of the ovaries (female reproductive system) in one fossil! If you saw Jingmai, you might not think she looks like a typical scientist. She wears bright clothes, has many piercings and tattoos, and likes to spend her free time dancing. But we all need to remember: there is no one way to look like a scientist. Despite what you might see on television, not all of us dress in white coats when we are working in the lab, or wear Indiana Jones hats when we are hunting for dinosaurs. Paleontologists are just people, and we have our own individual styles.

Many bird fossils are found alongside the feathered dinosaurs of Liaoning. The Liaoning birds are a snapshot of an ancient world. There is a variety of species, known from thousands of fossils that are usually found by farmers. Some of these birds lived in the trees, others on the ground, and others in and around the water, similar to ducks. Some of these still had teeth and long tails, retained from their *Velociraptor*-like ancestors, whereas others had the tiny bodies, huge breast muscles, stubby tails, and majestic wings of modern birds.

This is where things stood 66 million years ago. Many birds were there, gliding and flapping overhead, when *T. rex* and *Triceratops* were battling in North America, carcharodontosaurs were chasing titanosaurs south of the equator, and dwarf dinosaurs were hopping across the islands of Europe. And then they were witnesses to what came next – the instant that would erase almost all the dinosaurs. All except only a few of the most advanced, best-adapted, best-flying birds, which made it through the destruction and are still with us today.

14

Dinosaurs Die Out

Edmontosaurus

TIMELINE: End Cretaceous

66 million years ago

It was the worst day in the history of our planet. A few hours of terror that destroyed more than 150 million years of evolution and set life in a new direction.

T. rex was there to witness it. We can imagine what it might have been like.

When a pack of rexes woke up that morning – 66 million years ago, on what would go down as the final day of the Cretaceous Period – all seemed normal in their Hell Creek kingdom, the same as it had for generations. For millions of years.

Forests of evergreen trees stretched to the horizon, dotted with the bright flowers of palms and magnolias. The distant flow of a river was drowned out by the noises from a herd of *Triceratops*, several thousand strong.

As the pack of rexes readied themselves to go hunting, sunlight began to trickle through the canopy. It outlined the shadows of various small critters darting through the sky, some flapping their feathered wings and others gliding. Their chirps and tweets were beautiful, and could be heard by all the other creatures of the forest and river plains. There were armoured ankylosaurs and dome-headed pachycephalosaurs hiding in the trees, herds of duck-bills just beginning their breakfast of flowers and leaves, and raptors chasing little mammals and lizards through the brush.

Then things started to get weird.

For the last several weeks, the rexes had noticed a glowing thing in the sky, far off in the distance. It was a ball with a fiery rim, like a smaller version of the sun. This thing seemed to be getting larger every day. The rexes had no idea what it was.

But this morning, as the pack broke through the trees and emerged on to the riverbank, they could see that something was different. The fiery ball was gigantic. It filled the sky to the southeast with a strange orange light.

Then there was a flash. There was no noise, only a brief spark of yellow that lit up the whole sky, confusing the rexes for a moment. As they blinked their eyes, they noticed the glowing ball was now gone, and the sky was a dull blue.

And then their eyes went black. There was another flash, but this one was far more powerful. It lit the morning air like a fireworks display. One of the young rexes fell over, cracking her ribs. The rest of them stood frozen, trying to blink away the sparks that flooded their vision. But still, there was no sound to go with the light. In fact, there was no noise at all. By now, the birds and flying raptors had stopped chirping, and silence hung over Hell Creek.

208

The calm lasted for only a few seconds. Next, the ground beneath their feet started to rumble, then to shake, and then to flow. Pulses of energy were causing the ground to rise and fall, as if a giant snake were slithering underneath. Everything not rooted into the dirt was thrown upward, and then crashed downward, and then up and down again. The Earth's surface had turned into a trampoline. Small dinosaurs were catapulted into the sky, and even the biggest rexes were launched several feet off the ground. When they fell back down, the forces were more than enough to break bones, or even worse. By the time the shaking stopped, most of the rexes were lying on the ground. They had died.

Some of the rexes – and the other dinosaurs of Hell Creek – were able to walk away. As they did so, the sky began to change colour. Blue turned to orange, then to pale red. The red got darker. Brighter, brighter, brighter.

Then the rains came. But what fell from the sky was not water. It was beads of glass and chunks of rock, each one scalding hot. The pea-sized bits hit the surviving dinosaurs, burning into their flesh. Many of them couldn't endure the pain, and they too now died.

Meanwhile, as the bullets of glassy rock whizzed down from above, they were transferring heat to the air. The atmosphere grew hotter, until the surface of the Earth became an oven. Fires swept across the land. The once beautiful woodlands and river valleys were now flaming. Many dinosaurs died in the blaze.

All of this was happening so fast. It was no more than fifteen minutes since the *T. rex* pack was surprised by that first jolt of light. But by now they were all dead, as were most of the dinosaurs they lived with. But still, some animals had survived. Some of the mammals and lizards were hiding out underground, some of the crocodiles and turtles were protected underneath the water, and some of the birds were able to fly off to safer places.

Over the next hour or so, the rain of bullets stopped, and the air cooled. Calm once again settled over Hell Creek. It seemed like the danger was over, and many of the survivors came out of their hiding places. It was a sad scene. There was destruction everywhere, and although the sky was no longer red, it was getting blacker as it filled with smoke from the forest fires. The survivors must have thought that they had survived the apocalypse.

They were wrong. The clouds began to howl. The smoke in the atmosphere began to swirl into tornadoes. And then – whoosh – the wind charged across the plains and through the river valleys, blowing like a hurricane. Along with the wind was a noise, louder than anything these dinosaurs had ever heard. Then another. The survivors shrieked in pain, and many of the smaller critters hurried back into the safety of their burrows.

The Hell Creek survivors didn't know the whole story. Other parts of the world had many of the same problems. The mighty sauropods and carcharodontosaurs of South America, and the tiny dinosaurs living on the European islands, also had to deal with the fires, the winds, and the earthquakes. Some places had it even worse. Along much of the Atlantic Ocean coast, tidal waves as tall as the Empire State Building rushed on to the land. In India, volcanoes started to spew out rivers of lava. And worst of all, a zone of Central America was completely destroyed. The land was empty. It was as if everything – the dinosaurs, the other animals, the trees – was turned to dust.

In Hell Creek, things began to improve, little by little. As the morning gave way to afternoon, and then evening, the winds died down. The atmosphere continued to cool, and although there were a few smaller earthquakes, the ground was stable and solid. The fires burned away in the background. When night finally came, and this most horrible of days finally was over, many of the dinosaurs were dead. Maybe even most.

But some did stagger on, into the next day, the next week, the next month, the next year, and the next decades. It was not an easy time. For several years after that terrible day, the Earth turned cold and dark as the smoke and rock particles clouded the atmosphere and blocked out the sun. The darkness caused a winter that lasted for many years. Only the toughest and luckiest animals could survive.

It was also a difficult time for plants, as they need sunlight to power the photosynthesis that they use to make their food. As plants died, food chains collapsed, killing off many of the animals that had been able to endure the cold. Something similar happened in the oceans, where the death of tiny plankton took out the larger plankton and fish that fed on them, and in turn the giant reptiles at the top of the food chain.

The sun did eventually break through the darkness, as the smoke and other gunk was removed from the atmosphere by rainwater. But the rain was not able to remove billions of tons of carbon dioxide that had been blown up into the sky with the smoke. Carbon dioxide, or CO_2, is the nasty greenhouse gas that traps heat in the atmosphere, warming up the Earth. Thus, after a few years, the long winter gave way to global warming.

All these things – from the very first earthquakes and fires to the longer-term temperature changes – worked together to kill many species. They caused a mass extinction. Somewhere around 75 per cent of all species died. That means that three out of every four species alive at the end of the Cretaceous were wiped out.

A few hundred years after that dreadful day – a few thousand years at the absolute most – western North

America was a scarred landscape. What was once a thriving ecosystem of forests, alive with the hoofbeats of *Triceratops* and ruled by *T. rex*, was now quiet, and mostly empty. Here and there, a lizard scurried through the bushes, some crocodiles and turtles paddled in the rivers, and rat-sized mammals peeked out of their burrows. A few birds were still around, picking at seeds still buried in the soil, but all the other dinosaurs were gone.

It was the end of the Age of Dinosaurs.

So what was responsible for causing all the death and destruction? It started with that glowing ball in the sky. The ball was a comet or an asteroid, which came from outer space and collided with the Earth, hitting what is now the Yucatán Peninsula of Mexico. The asteroid was about 6 miles (10 kilometres) wide, or about the size of Mount Everest. It was probably moving at a speed of around 67,000 miles per hour (108,000 kilometres per hour), more than a hundred times faster than a jet airplane flies through the sky. When it slammed into the Earth, it impacted with the force of over 100 trillion tons of TNT, which is more energy than one billion nuclear bombs put together. It plowed some 25 miles (40 km) through the ground, and left a crater that was over 100 miles (160 km) wide.

This was not a normal event. Thankfully, humans have never experienced an asteroid impact anywhere

213

near as destructive. The monstrous asteroid that killed off the dinosaurs was one of the largest asteroids that has hit Earth over the last 500 million years.

DISCOVERING THE ASTEROID

Earth 45 seconds after the impact of the asteroid

How do we know that an asteroid hit the Earth and killed the dinosaurs? It's because of the work of an amazing geologist who is one of my heroes: Walter Alvarez.

His book *T. rex and the Crater of Doom* tells the story of how he discovered the asteroid. When I read it, I was captivated. I dreamed of one day going to the place where he found the rocks, which contained the clues that solved the

214

mystery: a gorge outside the medieval town of Gubbio, Italy. So I called Walter and asked him for more information. When I think back to that phone call, it was an unusual thing to do. I was fifteen years old; he was one of the world's most famous geologists. But he picked up the phone, and he was very nice. We chatted for a while, and then continued to stay in touch over email.

Five years later, I found myself in Italy. My college geology class was on a three-week field trip, to study the rocks and fossils of the area. We were staying in a small village high in the mountains, where there was a laboratory. On the first day we were given a tour, and as we passed through the library, I noticed a man looking at a map in the corner.

'I want you all to meet my friend and mentor, Walter Alvarez,' Alessandro Montanari, the director of the laboratory, announced to us. 'Some of you may have heard of him.'

I was shocked. Here was the eminent scientist I had been communicating with for years. After the tour, I snuck back to the library. Walter was still there, concentrating on the map. I introduced myself and was shocked a second time when he remembered our phone calls and emails.

'Get ready,' he told me. 'Because I'm taking your class to Gubbio. I'm going to show you where I discovered that an asteroid killed the dinosaurs.'

A few days later, Walter led us to the gorge.

Towering above us were walls of rosy pink limestone. Walter stepped up to the rocks and pointed to what looked like a thin crack. The crack was filled with another type of rock, softer and only about one centimetre thick. It was a layer of clay inside the limestone. This clay marked the moment the dinosaurs died. Below it was limestone from the Cretaceous Period, and above it was limestone from the time that came after, the Paleogene Period. The clay was essentially a bookmark between the world of the dinosaurs and the world that came later.

In the 1970s, Walter came to Gubbio to study the rocks to understand how the mountains of modern-day Italy had formed. But when he was there, he became fascinated by the fossils in the limestone. He learned about the work of an Italian student named Isabella Premoli Silva, who had carefully documented the fossils in the Gubbio gorge and realized something strange. The Cretaceous limestones below the clay layer were full of many fossils of microscopic ocean-living creatures called forams, of many shapes and sizes and species. But in the Paleogene limestones above the clay layer, there were very few forams, and they all looked the same. This confirmed that the clay layer represented a mass extinction. Many forams suffered at the same time as the dinosaurs.

But why? Walter wondered if the answer may be hidden in the clay itself. However, when he looked at the clay, it didn't seem very special. It wasn't a bizarre colour. It didn't smell rotten. It wasn't full of damaged fossils. So Walter called his dad for help.

His father, Luis Alvarez, was also a scientist, a physicist who years earlier had won the Nobel Prize. The father-and-son team worked together to analyze the chemical composition of the clay. They used powerful instruments to measure the amounts of different chemical elements – like oxygen, hydrogen, and others – inside the clay. They weren't prepared for what they found.

The clay contained an enormous amount of iridium. This is a very rare element on Earth, but it's common in outer space: on other planets, and in asteroids and comets. Maybe, Walter and Luis thought, some catastrophe from space killed the dinosaurs. It seemed like a silly idea, so they went to other places in the world where there were rocks formed at the end of the Cretaceous Period, and everywhere they went, they found iridium. So yes, something extraterrestrial must have happened 66 million years ago!

The Alvarez team presented their new theory in 1980. It immediately caused huge debates among scientists. Over the next decade, a lot of additional evidence turned up, showing that Walter and Luis were probably correct. The final clue that proved it was the discovery of a humongous crater, dated to exactly the end of the Cretaceous Period, in Mexico. The crater was mostly buried by the water of the Gulf of Mexico, so it took many years to find it and map it. But once that happened, the case was closed. An epic-sized asteroid really did hit the Earth 66 million years ago, right at the same time the non-bird dinosaurs disappeared.

But did the asteroid – and all the earthquakes, fires, and climate change that it caused – really kill the dinosaurs? Or were the dinosaurs dying out already? Paleontologists have spent the last four decades arguing about this question.

I am pretty confident the asteroid was responsible. If there was no asteroid – say, if the asteroid narrowly missed the Earth and flew right on by – then the non-bird dinosaurs would have kept on surviving.

The reason I'm so confident is that we know a lot about the dinosaurs that were living right before the asteroid hit. We know for certain that many dinosaurs were there when the asteroid struck. The story I told above is fiction: I don't know for sure whether a pack of *T. rexes* were killed by the asteroid in the exact way I describe. But I do know that there were earthquakes, fires, rains of glass bullets, a long winter, and global warming. All these things left evidence in the rocks. For example, we find the burnt wood left by the fires. I also know that *T. rex* – and the other Hell Creek dinosaurs like *Triceratops* – were there to experience it. We find their fossils in the very, very last rocks of the Cretaceous Period, right underneath the clay layer, full of iridium, that was created by the asteroid impact.

The Hell Creek fossils come from western North America, so we know many species of dinosaurs were still alive there when the asteroid hit. But what about other parts of the world? Over the last decade, paleontologists have discovered important new dinosaurs from the very end of the Cretaceous in Europe (Spain, France, and Romania) and South America (Brazil). Just like in North America, there were still many dinosaurs in these places, right until that fateful moment when the asteroid struck the Earth.

It is a tragic tale. Dinosaurs were prospering at the end of the Cretaceous. There were many species, some small and some big, some plant-eaters and some meat-eaters, some with horns or crests or dome-heads or long necks or bone-crushing jaws. They were living all over the world. We find so many of their fossils. And then the asteroid hits and the dinosaurs disappear. We never find their fossils in the Paleogene rocks that formed after the asteroid impact. Nobody has ever found a single bone, tooth, or footprint. This means the dinosaurs died off quickly, very soon after the asteroid collision.

Well, not all dinosaurs. The colossal sauropods,

bus-sized meat-eaters, horned and duck-billed plant-eaters, and many others died. But birds survived. There is no good answer for why the birds made it through. Maybe it was because they were smaller than most other dinosaurs, so they could hide more easily. Maybe it was because they could fly, so they could quickly move away from the worst of the destruction and find safer homes. Maybe it was because they had beaks that let them eat seeds: nutritious nuggets of food that can survive for a long time in the soil, long after trees have died and food chains have collapsed. Perhaps it was a combination of all these things. Or, I wonder, were the birds just lucky?

After all, so much about evolution – about life – comes down to luck. The dinosaurs got their chance to rise up after those terrible volcanoes 250 million years ago wiped out nearly every species on Earth. Then they had the good luck to sail through that second extinction at the end of the Triassic Period, which killed their crocodile competitors. Now the tables had turned. *T. rex* and *Triceratops* were gone. The sauropods would thunder across the land no more. But let's not forget about those birds – they are dinosaurs, they survived, they are still with us.

The dinosaur empire may be over, but the dinosaurs remain.

Epilogue

Torrejonia

Epilogue

At the start of most summers, I go to the desert of New Mexico. It's a bit of a break, following all the exam and essay marking I have to do at the end of the school year. I usually stay for a couple of weeks. By the end of my trip, the calm of the empty desert, and the spicy food we make every night in camp, have eased my stress.

But it's not a holiday. I'm here for business – to do what I've spent the last decade doing all over the world, in Polish quarries and on the tidal platforms of Scotland, in the shadows of Romanian castles or the outback of Brazil.

I'm here to find fossils.

Many of these fossils, of course, are dinosaurs. In fact, they were among the last surviving dinosaurs, ones that were living right before the asteroid hit. Back then, it appeared that dinosaurs would keep on ruling the world forever, as they had done for more than 150 million years. We find the bones of tyrannosaurs and sauropods, the skull domes that pachycephalosaurs used to headbutt each other, the jaws that horned and duck-billed dinosaurs sliced up plants with, and many raptor teeth. There were so many species living together, with no sign that things would soon go horribly wrong.

To be honest, however, I don't go to New Mexico *only* for the dinosaurs. That may seem strange, as I've spent most of my career on the trail of *T. rex* and *Triceratops*. But now what I'm trying to understand is what happened *after* the dinosaurs disappeared: how the Earth recovered and a new world was built. And New Mexico is the perfect place to solve these mysteries. Not only are there Cretaceous-aged dinosaur bones here, but there are fossils from the next interval of time: the Paleogene, which covers the first 40+ million years after the extinction.

I work in New Mexico with Tom Williamson, a curator at the natural history museum in Albuquerque. Tom has been collecting fossils in the badlands for twenty-five years. He often brings along his twin sons, Ryan and Taylor, who he taught to collect fossils when they were children. Often we are joined by Tom's students: young Native Americans of the Navajo tribe, whose families have lived on this land for generations. More recently, I've started to bring my own students too, including Sarah Shelley, who has become one of the world's experts on Paleogene fossils.

Tom has a skill that I lack, and one that is very useful for a paleontologist. He has a photographic memory. He can recognize each little hill and cliff in the desert, which all look the same to me. He can remember almost every fossil of the many thousands he's collected at these sites.

Fossils are littered across this landscape, constantly eroding out from the Paleogene rocks. But aside from a few bird bones here and there, these are not dinosaur fossils. They are the jaws and teeth and skeletons of the things that took over from the dinosaurs, the species that would go on to start the next great empire of Earth history. The empire that includes many of the most familiar animals of the modern world, and that also produced us.

Mammals.

Mammals got their start alongside the dinosaurs, living on Pangea more than 200 million years ago, during the Triassic Period. But mammals and dinosaurs then went their separate ways. While dinosaurs grew to colossal sizes and spread across the world, mammals remained in the shadows. They became good at eating different foods, hiding in burrows, and moving around quietly. Some even figured out how to glide through the trees and how to swim. All the while, they remained small. No mammal living with dinosaurs got bigger than a medium-sized dog.

In New Mexico, however, it is a different story. The fossils we collect belong to a great number of species. Some are tiny mouse-sized insect-eaters, not too different from the critters that lived under the feet of dinosaurs. But others are dog-sized burrowers, sabre-toothed flesh-eaters, and even cow-sized plant-eaters. They all lived during the earliest part of the Paleogene, just a few million years after the asteroid struck.

Not too long after the most destructive day in the history of Earth, the world had recovered. The temperature was neither freezing cold nor blistering hot. Forests of evergreen trees and flowering plants once again towered into the sky. Primitive cousins of ducks waited near the lakeside, while turtles paddled offshore, unaware of the crocodiles lurking underneath. But the tyrannosaurs and sauropods and duck-bills were gone, replaced by so many types of mammals.

Among the mammals that Tom and his crews have discovered is a skeleton of a puppy-sized creature, called *Torrejonia*. It has skinny limbs, and long fingers and toes. If you could have seen it alive, it probably would have looked quite cute and cuddly. Looking at its graceful skeleton, you can imagine it leaping through the trees, it skinny toes gripping on to the branches.

Torrejonia is one of the oldest primates, a member of the group of mammals that includes monkeys, apes, and humans. That means it is a cousin of ours. Another 60 million years of evolution would eventually turn *Torrejonia* into creatures that walk on two legs, have big brains, and read books: you and me.

It is weird to think about it, but if the asteroid never hit, if it never started that chain reaction of catastrophes that wiped out the dinosaurs, then the dinosaurs would probably still be here, and we would not. That's because primates got their opportunity to evolve only after the non-bird dinosaurs were wiped out.

But there is an even greater lesson in the dinosaur extinction. What happened at the end of the Cretaceous Period tells us that even the most dominant animals can go extinct, sometimes very suddenly. Dinosaurs had been around for more than 150 million years when the asteroid fell from the sky. There were probably many billions of dinosaurs, spread all across the world, from the valleys of Hell Creek to the islands of Europe, that woke up on that day 66 million years ago, confident of their place at the top of nature.

And then, literally in a moment, it ended.

Humans have now replaced dinosaurs as the dominant animals on Earth. But our actions are rapidly changing the planet around us. The world is getting hotter, storms are becoming more powerful, large forests and coral reefs are being destroyed, and pollution is harming many environments.

It leaves me uneasy, and a question sticks in my mind as I walk through the harsh New Mexican desert, seeing the bones of dinosaurs give way so suddenly to fossils of *Torrejonia* and other mammals.

If it could happen to the dinosaurs, could it also happen to us?

But another thought gives me hope. The dinosaurs couldn't stop the asteroid coming their way. Humans have much more power to change the world. We have big brains and the ability to work together. Hopefully we can stop ourselves, and the plants and animals that live around us, from going the way of *T. rex*, *Triceratops*, and the other extinct dinosaurs that used to rule the Earth.

Acknowledgments

I am ever grateful to my wife, Anne, for her support of my scientific research, travel, and writing. For this book, I am extra grateful, because Anne is a primary school teacher in Edinburgh, and she carefully read my drafts and gave me advice for writing for younger readers. She also told me when I was silly for using ridiculous technical words that even most adults wouldn't understand, writing paragraphs or chapters that were too long, and trying to cram too many tongue-twister dinosaur names into sentences.

My editors, Karen Chaplin at HarperCollins and Gaby Morgan at Macmillan, gave me the chance to write this book, and expertly guided me as I attempted a new type of narrative style for readers I've had little experience with.

I have a fantastic literary agent, Jane von Mehren. Jane heard me on the radio one day, and since then she hasn't stopped finding new opportunities for books and other projects. With hindsight, I can say that meeting Jane was one of the best things that has ever happened to me. Jane and her colleagues at Aevitas Creative Management (most notably Chelsey Heller, Erin Files, and Esmond Harmsworth) have masterfully handled every contract, and they've kept me motivated and happy about the world of publishing.

I only got the opportunity to write this book because of my adult pop-science book, *The Rise and Fall of the Dinosaurs*. So many people helped make that book a success, and without any of them, it would have quickly fallen into the bargain bin. Peter Hubbard was my astute and always-available editor for William Morrow (HarperCollins) in the USA, with assistance from the up-and-comer Nick Amphlett, and Robin Harvie and Ravi Mirchandani were my always-enthusiastic editors for Macmillan/Picador in the UK. The sales and marketing teams on both sides of the Atlantic did an outstanding job, both in getting publicity for the book and dealing with my anxiety and overenthusiasm: Maureen Cole, Bianca Flores, and Amelia Wood (USA); Rachel Mellor and Angela Robertson (UK); and Colleen Simpson (Canada). Elisa Montanucci at my Italian publisher, UTET, went far above and beyond, particularly in the pasta category. I will never forget the kindness exhibited by some of my idols, who blurbed the book before it was published: Steve Backshall, Peter Brannen, Richard Fortey, Ben Garrod, Neil Shubin, and Carl Zimmer. And of course: a huge thank-you to all of the journalists and reviewers who helped publicize the book, and most important, everyone who has bought, read, or otherwise picked up the book.

Neither this book, nor my adult book, would have been possible without my many friends and colleagues in the global community of dinosaur paleontologists. To everyone mentioned in these pages, and everyone else I have worked with: thank you.

My diverse and international group of students and postdocs at the University of Edinburgh constantly inspire me, and it makes me very proud to include some of them in this book: Hong-yu Yi, Shaena Montanari, Mark Young, Ornella Bertrand, Greg Funston, Sarah Shelley, Davide Foffa, Michela Johnson, Elsa Panciroli, Julia Schwab, Paige dePolo, Sofia Holpin, Zoi Kynigopoulou, Hans Püschel-Rouliez, Natalia Jagielska, Amy Muir, Joe Cameron, Moji Ogunkanmi, Matt McKeown, Fion Ma, Will Foster, Nikolai Hersfeldt, Kim Kean, Pei-Chen Kuo, Jules Walter. Thanks to all of my colleagues at the University of Edinburgh, particularly Professor Rachel Wood, and my current bosses, Professors Simon Kelley and Bryne Ngwenya, for allowing me time to write and explore my passion for science communication.

Thanks to my mentors: Paul Sereno, Mike Benton, and Mark Norell, and everyone else who has given me opportunities to study and describe dinosaurs. To my late friend and colleague Junchang Lü: 謝謝 (Xièxiè) and hope to see you again one day, but without donkey meat and baijiu.

My research wouldn't be possible without funding from many sources, including the National Science Foundation and Bureau of Land Management (and the US taxpayers who fund them), the National Geographic Society, the Royal Society and the Leverhulme Trust in the UK, and the EU-funded European Research Council and Marie Skłodowska-Curie Actions (and the European governments and taxpayers who fund them – and long may it continue in the UK, I hope).

And as always, a big thanks to my family. My parents, Jim and Roxanne, fostered my interest in dinosaurs and writing, my brother Chris got me obsessed with dinosaurs, and my brother Mike put up with it all. Peter, Mary, and Sarah Curthoys; Stephenie, Lola, and Luca: thank you too. And while I was doing revisions to this manuscript: my gorgeous son Anthony arrived!

To all of the teachers out there: keep doing what you're doing. This book is for you.

About the Author

Steve Brusatte is a paleontologist at the University of Edinburgh and a specialist on the evolution of dinosaurs. He has travelled the world digging up dinosaurs, named more than fifteen new species (including the tyrannosaur 'Pinocchio rex'), and published groundbreaking studies on the origin and extinction of dinosaurs. Steve has a bachelor's degree from the University of Chicago, a master's degree from the University of Bristol, and a PhD from Columbia University. He appears frequently on television and his work is covered often by the popular press. He is the author of the *New York Times* bestselling adult book *The Rise and Fall of the Dinosaurs* and has also written several books for children. A native of Ottawa, Illinois, Steve now lives in Edinburgh, Scotland.

233

Further Reading

This book is inspired by my adult pop-science book, *The Rise and Fall of the Dinosaurs* (William Morrow, 2018). A detailed list of sources for the specific dinosaurs and theories I write about can be found in that book. But there are so many dinosaur books for younger readers. Here are some additional resources that will provide more information on dinosaurs.

Dinosaurs, by Steve Brusatte (Quercus Publishing, 2008): This is a very large coffee table book that has profiles of around 100 dinosaur species, each one illustrated with colorful computer-generated artwork. Some of the dinosaurs – like *Microraptor* – are even illustrated at life size!

Day of the Dinosaurs, by Steve Brusatte (Wide Eyed Editions, 2016): This book was a collaboration with the creative artist Daniel Chester. We take the reader on a time-travelling adventure back to the Age of Dinosaurs, providing facts on the dinosaurs and their environments.

National Geographic Absolute Expert: Dinosaurs (National Geographic Kids, 2018): I served as the consultant for this book, which was written by Lela Nargi. The book tells the story of dinosaur evolution and how scientists dig up dinosaurs, and answers some of the big questions that people often have about dinosaurs.

Dinosaurs: The Most Complete, Up-to-Date Encyclopedia for Dinosaur Lovers of All Ages, by Thomas R. Holtz, Jr. (Random House, 2007): This is the ultimate dinosaur encyclopaedia, written by my colleague Thomas Holtz, a paleontologist who studies tyrannosaurs. It is expertly illustrated by Luis Rey, one of the most creative dinosaur artists in the world.

She Found Fossils, by Maria Eugenia Leone Gold and Abagael Rosemary West (CreateSpace Independent Publishing Platform, 2017): This book, written by two paleontologists who recently finished their PhD degrees, highlights the discoveries of female fossil hunters around the world, including many inspiring young scientists.

Dinosaur Atlas, by Anne Rooney (Lonely Planet Kids, 2017): This lively, well-illustrated book has up-to-date facts and information on the latest dinosaur discoveries in a very readable style. The young paleontologist David Button consulted on the book, ensuring the information is accurate.

Glossary

air sacs: balloon-like structures connected to the lungs that store oxygen to extend air supply

angiosperms: flowering plants

ambush predator: a carnivore that captures its prey by hiding or camouflaging itself before attacking

amphibians: a group of cold-blooded vertebrates such as frogs, toads, or salamanders

barbs: the extensions that project sideways from the central shaft of a feather

body fossil: an actual part of a plant or an animal that turns into stone

body plan: the distinctive features of a given species

carnivore: an animal that feeds on animal matter or meat

CAT scanner: a machine that uses X-rays to create a three-dimensional image of an internal object or body part

conglomerate: rock made up of pebbles and boulders glued together

coprolites: fossilized excrement

denticles: a bump or serration on a tooth

dinosaurs: a group of extinct herbivore or carnivore reptiles that roamed the Earth during the Mesozoic Era

dominant: residing at the top of an ecological community

ecosystems: a community of species living together and interacting with their environment

evolution: the process in which animals and other species slowly change over time to adapt to the world around them

extinct: no longer living

extinction line: a change in the type or quantity of fossils in a given sample of rock, which suggest that an extinction even took place

finite element analysis: the process of using computer models to predict what will happen to something when force is applied to it

fossils: the remains of ancient living things, such as plants and animals

geologist: a scientist who studies rocks

herbivore: an animal that feeds on plants

lava: hot liquid rock that has reached Earth's surface

link fossils: fossils that capture the evolution of one type of animal into another

magma: hot liquid rock under the Earth's crust

mammals: a group of warm-blooded vertebrates that can produce milk to feed their young

megavolcanoes: big cracks in the Earth, often miles

long, which continuously release lava

melanosomes: the capsules that hold pigment, which gives animals their colours

natural selection: a natural process in which the survival and reproductive success of individuals, or groups, best suited to their environment allows them to pass along their genes to the next generation

paleontologist: a scientist who studies fossils to understand what Earth was like in the distant past

Pangea: the name of the 'supercontinent' that once included the major landmasses of Earth before continental drift moved them to their modern locations

Panthalassa: the name of the single ocean that surrounded Pangea

plate tectonics: the process by which Earth's surface divided into plates and moved over millions of years

radioisotopic dating: a method used to determine the age of rocks by measuring the types of chemicals the rocks are made of

reptiles: a group of vertebrates including lizards, snakes, alligators, and dinosaurs

shale: rock hardened from ancient mud

sprawling: the limb posture of salamanders, frogs, and lizards in which their limbs stick out sideways from the body

trace fossil: a fossilized object that records the behavior of an animal or something that an animal produced

trackways: the sequence of handprints and footprints left by an animal

vertebrates: animals that have an internal skeleton made of bone

Index

243